D1020234

read 9/17

NATIONAL GEOGRAPHIC DIRECTIONS

ALSO BY SUSANNA MOORE

In the Cut
Sleeping Beauties
The Whiteness of Bones
My Old Sweetheart

I Myself Have Seen It

SUSANNA MOORE

I Myself Have Seen It: The Myth of Hawai'i

NATIONAL GEOGRAPHIC DIRECTIONS

NATIONAL GEOGRAPHIC
Washington, D.C.

Published by the National Geographic Society
1145 17th Street, N.W., Washington, DC 20036-4688

Text and photographs copyright © 2003 Susanna Moore
Map copyright © 2003 National Geographic Society

All photographs courtesy of the author except where noted

All rights reserved. No part of this book may be reproduced or transmitted in any form or by any means, electronic or mechanical, including photocopying, without permission in writing from the National Geographic Society.

Library of Congress Cataloging-in-Publication Data

Moore, Susanna.
    I myself have seen it : the myth of Hawaii / Susanna Moore.
        p. cm. -- (National Geographic directions)
    ISBN 0-7922-6528-9 (hc.)
    1. Moore, Susanna--Homes and haunts--Hawaii. 2. Novelists, American--20th
century--Biography. 3. Moore, Susanna--Childhood and youth. 4. Hawaii--Biography. 5.
Hawaii--History. I. Title. II. Series

    PS3563.O667Z465 2003
    813'.54--dc21
    [B]

                                                                    2003042198

One of the world's largest nonprofit scientific and educational organizations, the National Geographic Society was founded in 1888 "for the increase and diffusion of geographic knowledge." Fulfilling this mission, the Society educates and inspires millions every day through its magazines, books, television programs, videos, maps and atlases, research grants, the National Geographic Bee, teacher workshops, and innovative classroom materials. The Society is supported through membership dues, charitable gifts, and income from the sale of its educational products. This support is vital to National Geographic's mission to increase global understanding and promote conservation of our planet through exploration, research, and education.

For more information, please call 1-800-NGS LINE (647-5463), write to the Society at the above address, or visit the Society's Web site at www.nationalgeographic.com.

Interior design by Michael Ian Kaye and Tuan Ching, Ogilvy & Mather, Brand Integration Group

Printed in the U.S.A.

To my father

CONTENTS

I Myself Have Seen It

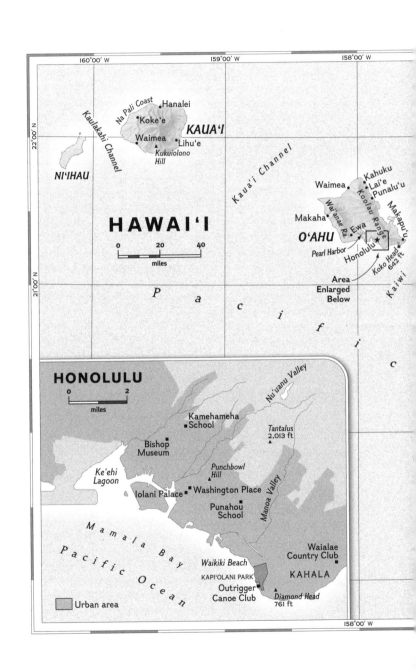

160°00' W 159°00' W 158°00' W

22°00' N

Na Pali Coast •Hanalei
•Koke'e **KAUA'I**
Waimea •Lihu'e
▲Kukuiolono
Hill

Kaulakahi Channel

NI'IHAU

Kaua'i Channel

Waimea •Kahuku
•Lai'e
Punalu'u
Wai'anae Ra. Koolau Range
Makaha• Makapu'u
O'AHU •Ewa
Pearl Harbor Honolulu Koko Head
642 ft

HAWAI'I

0   20   40
miles

Area
Enlarged
Below

Kaiwi

21°00' N

P   a   c   i   f   i   c

HONOLULU

0   2
miles

Nu'uanu Valley

Kamehameha
■School
Tantalus
2,013 ft
▲
Bishop
Museum

Ke'ehi
Lagoon

Punchbowl
Hill

Manoa Valley

■Iolani Palace ■Washington Place

Punahou
School

M a m a l a   B a y

Waialae
Country Club
■

P a c i f i c   O c e a n

Waikiki Beach

KAHALA

KAPI'OLANI PARK

Outrigger■
Canoe Club

Diamond Head
761 ft
▲

☐ Urban area

158°00' W

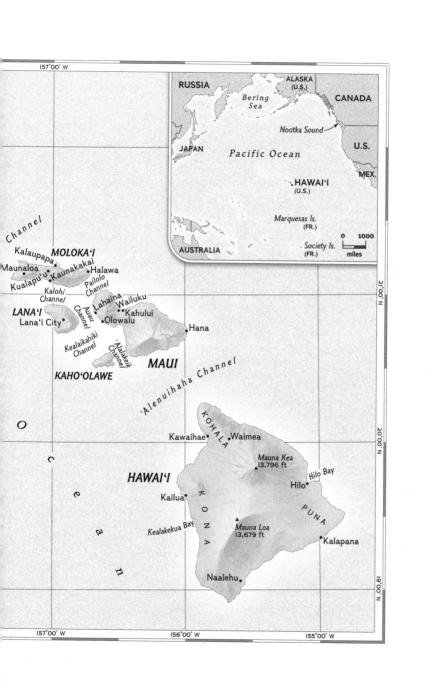

157°00' W

RUSSIA

ALASKA
(U.S.)

CANADA

*Bering
Sea*

Nootka Sound

JAPAN

U.S.

Pacific Ocean

MEX.

HAWAI'I
(U.S.)

Marquesas Is.
(FR.)

0   1000

AUSTRALIA

Society Is.
(FR.)

miles

Channel

Kalaupapa

MOLOKA'I

Maunaloa

Kaunakakai

Halawa

Kualapu'u

*Kalohi
Channel*

*Pailolo
Channel*

Wailuku

21°00' N

Lahaina

LANA'I

*Au'au
Channel*

Kahului

Lana'i City

Olowalu

Hana

*Kealaikahiki
Channel*

*'Alalakeik
Channel*

MAUI

'Alenuihaha Channel

KAHO'OLAWE

O

KOHALA

Kawaihae

Waimea

20°00' N

c

Mauna Kea
13,796 ft

Hilo Bay

HAWAI'I

K
O
N
A

Hilo

e

Kailua

a

Kealakekua Bay

P
U
N
A

Mauna Loa
13,679 ft

Kalapana

n

19°00' N

Naalehu

157°00' W

156°00' W

155°00' W

CHAPTER ONE

The Night Marchers

I grew up with people who believed unequivocally in the spirits. Simply to walk through the Tantalus forest where I lived as a child was to enter a kingdom of restrictions, blessings, and salutations. It was necessary to seek permission of the gods to bathe in a stream, to steal a fern, to cut a tree limb, to plant a bush, to eat Surinam cherries from the trees. I still beseech the protection of Mo'o, the great lizard-god, before bathing in a mountain pool, or, more accurately, I quietly let him know that I am hoping to refresh myself with a cold little swim and do not wish to disturb him. I don't want to awaken him should he be taking a nap. It is not his protection that I seek, but the indulgence of his indifference, which is rather what I want from most people as well as from dragons. While I do not really believe that I will endure endless calamities were I to fail

Moloka'i, 2002: Pu'u O Hoku

to ask permission of the wily fire goddess, Pele (who sometimes disguises herself as a withered crone, sometimes as a lovely woman), to walk across the black lava fields of the Big Island, it is oddly reassuring to think that I might, literally as well as metaphorically, be playing with fire.

If we take for myth an exaltation of the primeval reality that satisfies moral cravings as well as practical needs, my assumption of the myths of a race not my own, a race nearly annihilated by my kind, possesses a romanticism full of irony, an identification with the past, and a self-delighting pride at

SUSANNA MOORE

being a liminal participant in an authentic culture that continues, despite attempts to the contrary, to fear the ghostly night marchers and to honor the goddess of fire and her terrifying relatives. Despite those influences that proved threatening to the myths, folk customs, and history of the Hawaiian people in the nineteenth century, as well as the endless, vivid flow of foreigners—Portuguese, Spanish, English, Chinese, Japanese, Filipino, Samoan, and others—the myths have survived.

On the island of Moloka'i, a neighborhood storyteller, Harriet Ne, saw the spirits known as the night marchers as recently as 1958:

It is in the season called October and November that they come ... walking, walking, and chanting as they walk. When I was a child, one of my friends was a teacher at the school. On a certain evening ... the sound of chanting came to us. 'What is that, Harriet?' she asked. I knew at once what it was although I had never heard it before, but I said to her only, 'It's just someone chanting.' 'No,' she said, rubbing her arms. 'I am getting gooseflesh. Who is it really?' 'I think it is the night marchers going fishing,' I said. 'Let us go outside and watch.' The chanting came closer and closer. The first man was tall and strong, of the chief's class. All of them carried torches but the light did not shine on their faces, only on their bodies and legs. 'They will go down to the beach, following a pathway in a straight line,' I said. 'They will not turn to the right or to the left.' And so it was. Even as we watched, they continued down the hill to the house and then disappeared inside.... My brother was scornful of them.... Just as my aunt saw the marchers coming through the door, she snatched my brother away. As they went by, he tried to catch one of the legs of a fisherman, but the night marcher lifted his leg higher and kept marching.... I myself have seen it.[1]

On those nights when the marchers might be abroad, it is wise to leave open the front and back doors to facilitate their procession.

CHAPTER TWO

The Returning God

If we take for myth a theatrical ritual that transforms the mystery of the heroic into the sacred and magical, this particular myth begins with the arrival of one particular white man in January of 1778 to a chain of islands in the North Pacific.

Captain James Cook, aboard the H.M.S. *Resolution,* had left the Society Islands in the South Pacific at the beginning of the year. Short of food, having eaten most of the big sea turtle they'd caught a few days earlier, they were, therefore, much relieved to see the birds that signify the nearness of land and, soon after, the appearance of high peaks. On sailing closer, they saw native men in canoes. "We were in some doubt," wrote Cook in his journal, "whether or no the land before us was inhabited, this doubt was soon cleared up, by seeing some Canoes coming off from the shore toward the Ships."[1]

At the beginning of this third journey to the Pacific, Cook had been entrusted with secret instructions by the English government in the hope that he would find "'a North East, or North West Passage, from the Pacific Ocean into the Atlantic Ocean,'" and "'carefully ... observe the nature of the Soil and the Produce thereof; the Animals and Fowls that inhabit or frequent it ... And, if you find any Metals, Minerals of valuable Stones, or any extraneous Fossils, you are to bring home Specimens of each, as also of the Seeds of such Trees, Shrubs, Plants, Fruits, and Grains, peculiar to those Place, as you may be able to collect.'"[2]

Cook was eager to trade the men in canoes the nails and iron tools they seemed to desire so ardently in exchange for fruit, roots, fresh water (and valuable Stones). So many Indians, as Cook called them, came to the ships in canoes or swam alongside that by three o'clock in the afternoon, the white men had nothing more to give them. "I never saw Indians so much astonished at the entering a ship before, their eyes were continually flying from object to object, the wildness of their looks and actions fully express'd their surprise and astonishment at the several new objects before them."[3] Cook could not have known that there are no relative pronouns in the Hawaiian language; indeed no words to express having, possessing, deserving, or even existing, these constructs only expressed by attribution, frequently metaphoric. The Hawaiians felt free to take the objects that they so feverishly desired. "A simple iron nail," writes the Hon. R. M. Daggett in his introduction in 1887 to King Kalakaua's collection of Hawaiian myths, "was to them a priceless jewel, and every act and word betrayed an utter ignorance of everything pertaining to the white races."[4]

Eleven months later, having sailed as far north as Nootka Sound on the coast of America, Cook returned to the Islands. The night of the nineteenth of December was one of thunder, lightning, and rain in the North Pacific, the wind so squallish as to rip the main topsail of one of the ships. Cook took refuge in Kealakekua Bay (Pathway of the Gods) on the island of Hawai'i, sailing on what appeared to the excited natives to be small drifting islands planted with tall and slender trees that swayed with each surge of the sea. The mysterious floating islands had been first sighted in early December, and word quickly had been brought to Kalaniopu'u, the King of Hawai'i Island. There was no need for alarm; rather a reason for jubilant feasting. The floating islands were, after all, carrying the benevolent rain god, Lono, who had sailed away centuries before, come at last to bless the New Year's planting after his voyage of many years around the island. The early Hawaiian was much dependent on tubers—what Cook called roots—and, as foretold, the god brought with him the winter storms that ensured good planting.

Not only were the returning god and his attendants fair-skinned, as myth had also promised, but flying from the trees of the floating islands were pieces of white cloth similar to the banners on the long staff bearing the image of the god Lono in his *heiau,* or temple, on the southwest coast of the island. "An event so important and surprising as their arrival—the ships and the foreigners—the colour, dress, arms, language, manners, &c. of the latter, whom they regarded at first as superior beings, so powerfully affected the minds of the natives," wrote Rev. William Ellis, an English missionary from the Society Islands, "that the ordinary avocations of life were for a time suspend-ed.... The news of such an event rapidly spread through the islands and multitudes flocked from every quarter to see the return of Orono [Lono], or the motus (islands) as they called their ships."[5] Cook noted with approval the behavior of the Hawaiians: "No people could trade with more honesty than these people, never once attempting to cheat us.... Some indeed at first betrayed a thievish disposition, or rather they thought they had a right to any thing they could lay their hands upon but this conduct they soon laid aside."[6]

Each year in September, the Hawaiians put away their tools and ceased all planting and domestic tasks in anticipation of the great spring festival, the Makahiki, in honor of their absent god, Lono. Their customary activities of gathering and prepar-ing food, beating the bark of the mulberry tree to make *kapa* for garments and bedding, making ornaments of adornment and toys, plaiting thatch, ropes, baskets, nets, and sails were put aside to dance hula and sing chants. There were games of competition, boxing, and wrestling. War was prohibited. Deep-sea fishing was made impossible by rough seas.

Three hundred years earlier in Mexico, the approach by sea of the god Quetzalcoatl was also excitedly observed from shore: "As I walked on the seashore I saw a sort of hill mov-ing in the sea," reported the scout of the Emperor Montezuma. "We saw them fishing ... and then going back to two big towers, on to which they climbed. Their flesh was whiter than ours." After much consultation with his priests, the offering of more and more sacrificial victims, and the study of arcane texts, the emperor determined to fulfill the prophecy and prepared to welcome the returning god with great honors. Montezuma, a man of much learning, an astrologer and a philosopher, had known that the god Quetzalcoatl, who had been defeated in battle by the king of the gods, Smoking Mirror, would return one day to claim his rightful place. It was foretold by the Enchanters that he would come from the east in a strange vessel; he would be fair of skin. Until his return, however, he would be offered the best of each year's harvest during forty days of festival, at the end of which there would be sacrifices, the better to give the god new life and to ensure his resurrection.[7]

In Hawai'i, King Kalaniopu'u, known as the Island-Piercer, came that winter of 1778 in a flotilla of canoes to the *Resolution* to bestow on Cook royal offerings of red, yellow, and black feather capes and religious carvings, most of which now reside in the British Museum. A chieftain in the king's retinue was the young Kamehameha, known for his strength and his silence. He "seldom smiled or engaged in the manly sports so attractive to others, and his friends were the few who discerned in him a slumbering greatness."[8] According to James King, Cook's second lieutenant, the high priest Koah "approached Captain Cook with great veneration, and threw over his shoulder a piece of red cloth, which he had brought along with him. Then stepping a few paces back, he made an offering of a small pig, which he held in his hand, whilst he pronounced a discourse that lasted for a considerable time. The ceremony ... appeared to us ... to be a sort of religious adoration."[9]

It was a particularly splendid homage paid Cook, as well as some of his officers, only a few of whom were made ill at ease.

> Whilst Captain Cook was aloft, in this aukward
> situation, swathed round with red cloth, and with
> difficulty keeping his hold amongst the pieces of
> rotten scaffolding, Kaireekeea and Koah began their
> office, chanting sometimes in concert, and some-
> times alternately. This lasted a considerable time;
> at length Koah let the hog drop, when he and the
> Captain descended together. He then led him to
> the images before mentioned, and having said
> something to each in a sneering tone, snapping his
> fingers at them as he passed, he brought them to
> that in the centre, which, from its being covered in
> red cloth, appeared to be in greater estimation than
> the rest. Before this figure he prostrated himself,
> and kissed it, desiring Captain Cook to do the same;
> who suffered himself to be directed by Koah
> throughout the whole of the ceremony.[10]

Rev. William Ellis, visiting nearly fifty years later, writes
that the idol's head "has generally a most horrid appearance, the
mouth being large and ... extended wide, exhibiting a row of
large teeth ... adapted to excite terror rather than inspire confidence.... The effect ... produced on the minds of those early visitors, by what they saw during their transient stay among the
islands, was heightened by all the attractions of novelty, and all
the complacency which such discoveries naturally inspire."[11]
Although the god of war thrived on human sacrifice, the
Englishmen were not alarmed. Nor, despite their understandable
ignorance of Hawaiian mythology, were they overly surprised by

HONOLULU ACADEMY OF ARTS, GIFT OF MRS. C. M. COOKE, 1927

Captain Cook meets with Hawaiian nobility under an effigy of the god Lono.

the extraordinary reverence with which they were received. "He [Captain Cook]," writes historian Bernard Smith in *Imagining the Pacific,* "could not have known as he left the island of Bora Bora that he would discover another great Polynesian society in the north Pacific unknown to Europeans, and that there he would be received as the very incarnation of a god of peace, as the returning god, Lono, the god of carnival, of the Makahiki festival. So it was that Cook was received, as few men have been, into an alien culture in a fashion that accorded with his own personal and most innermost desire."[12]

On his equally momentous arrival in Mexico in the sixteenth century, the Spanish conquistador, Hernán Cortés, was given a necklace of golden shrimps—some say it was strung with golden crabs—which Montezuma condescended to hang around Cortés's neck with his own hands, saying, "Ah, these days ... I have been anxious, watching for you, waiting to see you appear from your hidden place among the clouds and mists. For the ... ancestors told that you would appear, that you would return to sit on your mat, your stool. Now it has come true; you have returned. With toil, with weariness, you have reached us at last. Welcome to this land." On realizing that his world had been overturned and the gods displaced, Montezuma sent Cortés more and more gold, saying mournfully to his priests, "We have swallowed the poison. Nevertheless, some means may yet be found."[13] Bernal Diáz del Castillo, one of Cortés's captains, writing half a century later in *The Conquest of New Spain*, praised Montezuma, whom the Spanish much admired. The emperor made "a very good speech, saying that he was delighted to have such valiant gentlemen as Cortés and the rest of us in his house and his kingdom ... [as] we must truly be the men about whom his ancestors had long ago prophesied, saying that they would come from the direction of the sunrise to rule over these lands."[14] Diáz does not make note of Cortés's vanity or curiosity, which were very great, only his sly politeness in accepting Montezuma's offer of his throne on "our lucky and daring entry into the great city of Mexico on 8th November 1519. Thanks to our Lord Jesus Christ for it all."[15]

Captain Cook's willingness to make a reverential tour of the heiau in honor of the Hawaiians' gods did not prevent him, however, from sending his men to take the wooden palings of the temple enclosure to use as firewood. In pulling up the fencing, the sailors also gratuitously carried off several wooden images to burn, a defilement that understandably alarmed the Hawaiians. Upon learning this, Cook quickly made amends, sending his lieutenant to the chief priest, who asked only that his one staff with the little image of the god be returned. Fortunately, Lono was a benevolent god and would not punish the sailors.

Soon after this misunderstanding, Kalaniopu'u and his high chiefs sent for news of the white god's departure to begin his ritual tour of the island, and were much relieved to be told that Cook's ships were presently to sail north out of Kealakekua Bay. Cook, however, was compelled to return on the eighth of February 1779, five days after his departure, when a winter storm damaged the rotten driftwood splints he had applied to his weakened masts in Nootka Sound during the previous year's expedition to America.

Cook was disappointed upon returning to find the bay unusually quiet. It was the time of dark weather and the rain would continue until the end of February when sweet potatoes would again be planted on the slopes of Mauna Loa, and taro in the water meadows. Unlike his triumphant reception the month before, the Hawaiians were not eager to come to the big ships. There was scant trading—no small pigs, no roots—and it was assumed that for some unknown reason the natives had been proscribed by their king from attending the big ships.

Kalaniopu'u, who possessed the protection of the shark-gods—his own shark hula with its terrible moans and gestures contained the salutation, "You are a white-finned shark riding the crest of the wave, O Kalaniopu'u: a tiger shark resting without fear, a rain quenching the sun's eye-searing glare, a grim oven glowing underground"[16]—came humbly to Cook to inquire of his mysterious return. The sacrifices had been fastidiously performed, the kava brewed, the *meles* (songs) composed and chanted. The Hawaiians had given the god and his men everything that they desired, generously emptying their longhouses of stores to keep the god happy. "The whole Island was land under requisition," wrote Rev. William Ellis, "to supply their wants, or contribute to their satisfaction. Hence the immense quantity of provisions, presented by Kalaniopuu; the dances, &c. with which they were entertained."[17] When told that the floating islands had returned for new tree masts, Kalaniopu'u appeared "very much displeased."

The Hawaiian, like the Mexican, is the descendant of migrating tribes from northeast Asia, some of whom crossed the Bering Strait to North America in the late Paleolithic and Neolithic eras, and others who moved southward to spread across the Pacific by way of New Guinea and the Antipodes, carrying their gods with them. The Hawaiian was not unique in believing that invisible spirits determined his destiny. These fearsome powers, unfortunately not always well disposed as shown by tidal waves and volcanic eruptions and plagues, were in need of placation if they were to continue to bestow their desultory blessings.

As in many cultures, the religious rites necessary to appease the spirits were a highly theatrical reenactment of the slaying of the primordial god first killed in order to bring the world into existence, and who must be killed each year in order to safeguard the return of life. The sacrificed god survives in his creatures— plants, animals, rocks—and he is, of course, transformed into man himself. The repetition of the ritual reassures man that something exists absolutely, and that that something is sacred. The sacrifice of a little pig to Cook is a reminder of that first life-giving murder. "Its repetition has no other meaning," writes philosopher Mircea Eliade, "than to recall the divine exemplary act that gave birth to everything that exists on Earth today." If all sacrifice is an act of veneration in honor of the first murder then "in one way or another, men are always eating the divinity."[18] A text of Meister Eckhart, a German mystic of the fourteenth century, reads, "Here in time we make holiday because the eternal birth ... is now born in time, in human nature. St.Augustine says this birth is always happening."[19]

The Makahiki ceremonies in honor of Lono began with the first sighting from the god's heiau of the Pleiades rising at sunset (it is still traditional on New Year's Day to offer the salutation, *Hauoli Makahiki Hou*). It is an intrinsic part of the myth of the returning fertility god that a mock battle be held in which the reigning king-god or his proxy is each year defeated until the following year's festival of death and rebirth. The enactment of the ritual is essential in order for man to know that "what he is about to do has already been done ... [helping] him to overcome doubts as to the result of his undertaking."[20]

The man chosen by Kalaniopu'u to represent the god Lono came ashore in a canoe where he was met by warriors who ceremoniously threw their weapons at him. He was not meant to be harmed, and a spear with its point wrapped in kapa was pressed to his body. Lono, defeated symbolically, would then bestow to Kalaniopu'u, the god's surrogate and mortal self, the kingship for yet another year until the god appeared once again to enact their struggle. (This theory of the returning fair-skinned god is held in disfavor by recent historians who see it as an imperialist interpretation that belittles the shrewdness and sophistication of a native people who, in this view, did not ever entertain fantasies of birth and resurrection, and apparently possessed no unconscious, collective or otherwise.)

All went as expected that winter until the god changed the rules. After Cook had surprised the Hawaiians by returning to Kealakekua Bay, one of his cutters was stolen. To ensure the safety of his ships and his men, given the state of the increasingly anxious Hawaiians, Cook unwisely determined to take Lono's avatar, Kalaniopu'u, hostage, as Cortés took Montezuma his prisoner, thus ensuring the revolt of the people. The Hawaiian *ali'i*, or nobility, were held in such importance that merely to gaze upon them meant death, requiring the highest chiefs to travel only by night. Cook's attempt to take the king hostage was an act of usurpation, even if he were acting like a god. "In the Pacific," writes Bernard Smith, "Cook had to play at being, as best he could, Adam Smith's god. If the laws of property essential to a free market economy were transgressed and a goat stolen, an act of the god must descend upon the whole community. If a law is not understood as a natural law, the best thing to do, if you possess the power of a god, is to make it seem like one."[21]

As intended, Kalaniopu'u and his chieftains believed themselves punished. The god had been behaving in an increasingly erratic way, it is true, refusing to share his gifts of food with the chiefs and priests as was the custom, but Cook's attempt to seize the king was an extreme deviation from tradition. Did the high chiefs begin to doubt Cook's divinity, as Montezuma's lords began to doubt Cortés? That the Hawaiians dared to kill Cook in an awkward struggle on the beach would suggest that Cook had begun to lose some of his mana, or spiritual power, as good a reason as any for murder. For Cook, "movement was freedom. In movement he realised his innermost nature; to remain at home was, for him, to be a captive.... Unlike the old navigators, he publishes his voyages: freedom of trade is dependent upon freedom of knowledge.... Almost a century before Carlyle defined this new kind of self-dependent genius that the times had need of as 'the transcendent capacity for making trouble,' Cook had already demonstrated the new type."[22]

"Our unfortunate Commodore, the last time he was distinctly seen," wrote Lieutenant King, who was to take command of the *Resolution* upon Cook's death, "was standing at the water's edge, and calling out to the boats to cease firing, and to pull in."[23] In the confusion, Cook was struck on the head by a warrior's club and fell with his face in the water. As told by others, however, Cook was stabbed in the back with a crude dagger made from the very iron that the English had traded to the Hawaiians. "Cook had taken with him iron from a Birmingham factory that, when fashioned into daggers, was used to cut him down on Kealakekua beach," writes Smith. "For when Cook, this man of peace, attempted for the last time to take a Pacific chieftain hostage—dealing once again in the coercive market in which captives were exchanged for stolen goods—the hidden hand of

Kukalimoku, the Hawaiian god of war, struck him down and four of his marines. Cook had committed the fatal error of returning to the island when peace no longer reigned there, not even in myth."[24]

Fifty years later, Rev. William Ellis found several of the Hawaiians who had witnessed Cook's death.

> 'The foreigner,' they say, 'was not to blame; for, in the first instance, our people stole his boat, and he, in order to recover it, designed to take our king on board his ship, and detain him there till it should be restored.... Kapena Kuke (Capt. Cook's name is thus pronounced by the natives) and Taraiopu [Kalaniopu'u] our king were walking together toward the shore, when our people, conscious of what had been done, thronged around the king, and objected to his going any further. His wife also joined her entreaties that he would not go on board the ships. While he was hesitating, a man came running from the other side of the bay, entered the crowd almost breathless, and exclaimed, "It is war!—the foreigners have commenced hostilities, have fired on a canoe from one of their boats, and killed a chief." ... The captain seemed agitated, and was walking toward his boat, when one of our men attacked him with a spear: he turned, and with his double-barrelled gun shot the man who struck him.... [Cook] was turning again to speak to us, when he was stabbed in the back with a

pahoa; a spear was at the same time driven through his body; he fell into the water, and spoke no more.' We have sometimes asked them what inducement they had to steal the boat, when they possessed so many canoes of their own.... They did not take it to transport themselves from one island to another, for their own canoes were more convenient, and they knew better how to manage them; but because they saw it was not sewed together, but fastened with nails. These they wanted ... to make fish-hooks with.[25]

Cook was buried with the greatest honor. His corpse was nestled in a few inches of sand over which a pyre was lighted to burn away the flesh without searing the bones, which were then carefully wrapped in kapa and placed in his own temple of Lono where he was worshiped for generations until the relics were swept away, or stolen, or buried in secret with other old beliefs.

CHAPTER THREE

The Europeans

Despite the myth of the Birmingham dagger (if it is not historically true, it is metaphorically true), Captain Cook was not the first European to bring iron to the Sandwich Islands. He had noted the incredulity of the Hawaiians at their first sight of it, but there already were bits and pieces of iron amongst the natives' tools. Cook surmised that the little iron the natives did possess had been scavenged from shipwrecks—in the Society Islands, the natives so prized nails that they planted them in the ground like potatoes in the hope that they would grow.[1]

It is now thought probable that the Hawaiian Islands were discovered as early as 1555 by the Spanish captain, Juan Gaetano, on his way from the west coast of Mexico to the Spice Islands. Although Gaetano did not trouble to claim the islands as had been done in the West Indies and the Philippines, the

Spanish government still holds one of his manuscript charts as proof of his discovery.[2] Hawaiian myth hints at the landing of small parties of white men at the end of the sixteenth century, but the men were not well enough remembered, or important enough, despite the extraordinary things they brought with them, to render Cook's arrival two hundred years later anything less than a religious visitation for which new myths were composed. If myth, inextricably bound to religion, geography, and history, is cherished from generation to generation, it is also sometimes abandoned and forgotten.

In his voluminous history of the Polynesian race, Judge Abraham Fornander, a Swedish student of theology who gave up his calling to take ship on a whaler, and was later to settle in the Islands and marry a Hawaiian woman, believed that the survivors of shipwreck had another profound effect on the Hawaiian. As the similarities between Hawaiian myth and Old Testament history—the Creation, the Forbidden Fruit, the Flood, Joseph and his brothers—cannot be fully explained, Fornander held that the foreigner also brought the Old Testament with him. "Some shipwrecked people ... had obtained sufficient influence to introduce these scraps of Bible history into the legendary lore of [the Hawaiian] people.... The other hypothesis is ... a body of the scattered Israelites had arrived at these islands direct, or in Malaysia, before the exodus of 'the Polynesian family' and thus imparted a knowledge of their doctrines, or the early life of their ancestors, and of some of their peculiar customs.... It probably descended to the Chaldeans, Polynesians, and Hebrews alike, from a source or people anterior to themselves, of whom history now is silent."[3]

Although the Spanish are suspected of bringing the mosquito from Mexico in 1826, it is generally held to be true that it was Cook who introduced the "Venereal Complaint" to the Islands. He was well aware of the danger of communicating it to the natives and wrote orders that "no women [of the Sandwich Islands] on any account whatever ... be admitted on board the Ships ... and none who had the venereal upon them should go out of the Ships.... I am much afraid that ... there will be found some who will endeavour to conceal this disorder, and there are some again who care not to whom they communicate it." Cook made this entry in his journal during a visit to the island of Kaua'i. By the time of his return on the third voyage and his stay in Kealakekua Bay ten months later in January 1779, he was again to issue orders that Hawaiian women were forbidden to board the ships. "But the evil I meant to prevent by this I found has already got amongst them."[4] (A little more than 150 years later, the Honolulu Board of Health reports that in 1945, another year of high naval presence, incidence of the Venereal Complaint was 2,826 per 100,000 population.)[5]

"Cook on his third voyage grew more and more aware in his grand role as Enlightenment Man that he was involved in contradictions that he could not resolve," writes Bernard Smith. "He had come to the Pacific to spread the blessings and advantages of civilised Europe.... Cook [had] increasingly realised that wherever he went he was spreading the curses much more liberally than the benefits of European civilisation. The third voyage records not only his death but, before that, his loss of hope."[6]

CHAPTER FOUR

The Great King

In 1790, a middle-aged boatswain from Yorkshire named John Young left the American ship, the *Eleanora,* which was under the command of Capt. Simon Metcalfe, to go ashore at Kealakekua Bay on the island of Owyhee (Hawai'i) to shoot birds, unaware that only days earlier the schooner *Fair American,* also owned by Metcalfe, had been captured by the Hawaiians. The entire crew and the captain of the *Fair American,* who was Metcalfe's young son, Thomas, had been killed except for the mate, Isaac Davis. This attack was made in revenge for a gratuitous massacre a few weeks earlier at Olowalu, when Simon Metcalfe had recklessly opened fire on hundreds of Hawaiian women and children and men trading fruit and vegetables from canoes, in retaliation for the earlier theft by the natives of a dinghy and the murder of one of

Metcalfe's sailors, found by the surprised Hawaiians asleep in the bottom of the boat.

So that the vindictive Metcalfe would not instigate more killing, Kamehameha, Kalaniopuʻu's nephew and successor as king of Hawaiʻi Island, enjoined the strictest secrecy upon his people, forbidding them to speak of the retaliatory killing of the American sailors, and establishing a *kapu,* or taboo, to prevent all canoes from putting to sea. So rigid was the kapu that violation would bring ritual strangulation. Kamehameha, a warrior of great size, was possessed of high intelligence and, what seems to have been rarer, an even temper—Rev. William Ellis writes that "he has been called the Alfred of the Hawaiians; but he appears rather to have been their Alexander."[1] At Kamehameha's birth, in 1758, a rival high chief had determined to kill the infant, but Kamehameha's mother had spirited him away, traveling by darkness to an isolated valley on the remote Kohala coast of northeast Hawaiʻi. The child remained hidden for five years (the translation of his name is "the lonely one"), attended only by the warrior, Kekuhaupiʻo, who was his tutor and companion (as in many legends of young princes and their teachers—Arthur and Merlin, Achilles and Phoenix, Krishna and Arjuna). Kamehameha's claim to the kingship was less valid than that of other high chiefs, particularly that of his cousin, and upon the death of Kalaniopuʻu he had fought for ten years to claim the island as his own. To ensure his succession, he had also married his cousin's sister.

Some historians have suggested that Kamehameha needed an instructor in the use of his small arsenal of captured cannons and guns. With the king's royal kapu, John Young could not return to his ship, and the impatient Captain Metcalfe soon sailed away to the east, leaving Young and Isaac Davis in the hands of the king. Five years later, it was with Young's tactical help (and his mastery of firepower) that Kamehameha and his army of sixteen thousand warriors defeated the chiefs of all the islands but Kaua'i to create the first unified Hawaiian empire. So powerful had John Young become that no decision of statecraft, no business arrangement was made without the approval of the king's spokesman. Despite the myth that the land itself was sacred and thus could not be owned, Kamehameha gave to Young thousands of acres on the Kona coast of Hawai'i.

On the night of May 7, 1819, as the First Company of American missionaries was bearing down on the Islands, the great king lay dying. The historian Kamakau tells us that "John Young put his arms around (the king's) neck and kissed him."[2] The king "took a morsel of food and swallow of water. He had neither strength nor desire for more.... Then chief Kaikioewa asked him for a last word, perhaps to give them an instruction. He told his king, 'We are all here, your younger brothers, your chiefs, your foreigner (John Young). Give us a word.' The words the ... king gave to the small but prestigious group were, 'Endless is the good that I have given you to enjoy.'"[3] The good was to last but a year.

In keeping with the tradition of burial, the body of Kamehameha the Great was taken to his heiau and given to the priests. As with Captain Cook's body, the corpse was washed and wrapped in a shroud of green taro and banana leaves, laid in a shallow pit, covered lightly with sand, and burned for ten days. The priests scraped what seared flesh remained from the bones and dropped it into the ocean as ritual required. The bones were lain in a specially woven sennet basket and taken in great secrecy to a burial cave.

Five years ago, a friend of my earliest childhood, Nancy Johnson, was swimming at the Mauna Kea Hotel in Kawaihae, near the place of Kamehameha's birth and rumored to be the place of his burial, when she saw at sea level the entrance to a cave, visible only at low tide. She swam into the cave. It was as dark as night inside the cave, but for a scant moment of sunlight each time the ocean receded, leaving the entrance uncovered. The water was deep and the cave rose to a height of ten feet. In one of the intervals of light, she saw, to her astonishment, a long wooden canoe wedged onto a natural shelf near the dome of the cave. What appeared to be sticks wrapped in kapa were inside the canoe, as well as long spears. As the water was rising with the turn of the tide, there was not enough time to climb onto the ledge to look inside the canoe. A week later, after swearing me to secrecy, we swam along the coast at low tide, looking for the entrance to the cave, but we could not find it. She has looked for it many times since, but she has never seen it again. The Hawaiians say, "The morning star alone knows where Kamehameha's bones are guarded."[4]

CHAPTER FIVE

The Kapu

If we take for myth the means by which the transcendent idea of existence is both reaffirmed and protected, Queen Ka'ahumanu, Kamehameha the Great's favorite consort, committed an act of nihilistic subversion when she convinced the dying king's heir to overturn the gods. At Ka'ahumanu's prodding, Liholiho, who was to become Kamehameha II, broke one of the most sacred of all the kapus by eating with her. "Liholiho ... suddenly, and in the presence of a large concourse of horrified natives, broke the ... tabus of his religion by partaking of food from vessels from which women were feasting, and the same day decreed the destruction of every temple and idol in the kingdom."[1] (Was the Queen driven by fury? Necessity? Why did she refuse the inner darkness? It must have been hard for her—the sadness, the defiance, the refusal that gave her form and existence.) King

David Kalakaua writes in 1887 that with the breaking of the kapus, "Feasts were at once provided, and men and women ate together indiscriminately. The tabu foods of palace and temple were voraciously eaten by the masses, and thousands of women for the first time learned the taste of flesh and fruits which had tempted their mothers for centuries."[2] The observance of the eating kapu, like all ritual, had been an act of worship. If a woman, even a queen, were caught eating kapu foods (bananas, the *ulua* fish, the *kumu* fish, pig, coconut, fowl, turtle, and shark—in other words, just about everything but tubers), she would be put to death. "The tabu," wrote the historian Kamakau, "was a fixed law for chiefs and commoners, not because they would die by eating tabu things, but in order to keep a distinction between things permissible to all people and those dedicated to the gods."[3]

"[The tabu applied to] ... idols, temples, persons, and names of the king, and members of the reigning family; the persons of the priests; canoes belonging to the gods; houses, clothes, and mats of the king and priests; and the heads of men who were the devotees of any particular idol," wrote Rev. William Ellis. "Sometimes an island or a district was tabued, when no canoe or person was allowed to approach it.... The seasons generally kept tabu were ... on the approach of some great religious ceremony; immediately before going to war; and during the sickness of chiefs.... There was a tabu kept thirty years, during which the men were not allowed to trim their beard."[4]

Lovely glades and mountain streams, and little pools filled with the freshwater shrimp much favored by the ali'i were declared kapu. During periods of kapu, no fires could be lit. Cats were muzzled and chickens were thrown into covered calabashes to keep them silent. The king's excrement was borne away by his most trusted chief and destroyed in secret not because of modesty or shame, or even hygiene, but because an evildoer might use it for sorcery. If you were so reckless as to raise your head as the big calabash containing the king's nail clippings was borne past, you were taken to the heiau and strangled to death. Only at the death of the king were the people allowed to break the rules with impunity. They joyously burned, looted, and murdered, and the women offered themselves as prostitutes— but only until the burial of the king was complete, when order, with its rigid system of kapu, was effortlessly restored.

The kapu had practical, as well as symbolic usage, most often in the interest of the ali'i who maintained power through exclusion and fear. A taboo existed in order to be transgressed. Violence, ritualized violence, lay deep at the center of things. To be an ancient Hawaiian was to be terrified most of the time. It is a modern idea, as well as a sentimental one, that to live in a subconscious state is poetic. This stanza is from the creation chant, the "Kumulipo":

> *Fear falls upon me on the mountain top*
> *Fear of the passing night*
> *Fear of the night approaching*
> *Fear of the pregnant night*
> *Fear of the breach of law*
> *Dread of the place of offering and the narrow trail*
> *Dread of the food and the waste part remaining*
> *Dread of the receding night*[5]

In convincing Liholiho to abolish the kapus that spring of 1819, Ka'ahumanu usurped the role of the ancient gods in the lives of the people and, quite directly, given the irony of her timing, made them susceptible to and even eager for the new myth headed their way with the first Protestant missionaries. "Within a few weeks idols, temples, altars, and a priesthood which had held prince and subject in awe for centuries were swept away, leaving the people absolutely without a religion.... The abolition of the tabu, which had made them slaves to their chiefs and priests, and held their fathers in bondage for centuries, was hailed with so great a joy by the native masses that they did not hesitate when called upon to consign the priesthood and their gods to the grave of the tabu."[6]

Although some of the priests and their followers refused to repudiate the gods, continuing to perform the rituals in secret, few Hawaiians were able to hold onto their beliefs. It cannot have escaped their notice that the sailors and merchants did not keep to the Hawaiians' rigid tabus and yet went unpunished by the priests, as well as the gods. "When the national idolatry was ... abolished in the year 1819," writes Mr. Ellis, "several priests of Pele denounced the most awful threatenings, of earthquakes, eruptions, &c. from the gods of the volcanoes, in revenge for the insult and neglect then shewn them by the king and chiefs. But no fires afterward appearing ... some of the people have been led to conclude, that the gods formerly supposed to preside over volcanoes had existed only in their imagination."[7] Sarah Lyman, the wife of the missionary, Rev. David Lyman, came upon an old believer in 1832, thirteen years after Liholiho destroyed the gods by sitting down to eat with his father's wife. She wrote in a letter: "A man ... was not long since detected in worshipping a God of his own hands making. He was arrested by authority from a chief and brought to this place. Early this morning I was called to the door to see his god, and was surprised to find it was nothing more than a handful of earth, a small stone, a pepper pod, several kinds of roots, and a few caster beans. These he kept deposited in a calabash and paid homage to it."[8]

It was not uncommon in my childhood to come across pieces of unearthed artifacts and images and, more often, the abandoned stone shrines, less friable but more melancholy, erected to fishing gods or trees, and stone tools, and the round stone disks called *'ulumaikas* which were used in a game like bowls. Such discoveries evoked in us a fear that we, like some of the Hawaiians, were compelled to hide, although in our case it was to prevent the anthropologists at the Bishop Museum (built in 1899 by Princess Bernice Pauahi), from hearing of our find and claiming it for the museum. One of my brothers stumbled over a smooth gray stone poi-pounder that was hundreds of years old, but hid it so well in the jungle of vines behind our garden that it was lost yet again.

CHAPTER SIX

The Children

The little bands of American altruists who came in twelve successive companies from 1820 to 1844 were possessed of their own particular myth of death and resurrection, albeit a Christian one, which they deemed so powerfully true as to happily relinquish ties to custom, family, and place (the men were graduates of Yale and Amherst and Williams), and to dedicate their lives to saving from perdition thousands of black natives in an isolated group of volcanic islands in the middle of the Pacific. Although John Dominis Holt, a descendant of Queen Lili'uokalani's consort, John Owen Dominis, who was said to be the son of a "dashing sea captain of Yugoslav ancestry and a Boston bluestocking," was to describe the missionaries as "unctuous and often inaccurate zealots [who did not] realize ... that irreparable harm they were doing to Hawaiian self-esteem by these wanton attacks upon the way of life of their ancestors,"[1] the missionaries themselves, who were not without doubt concerning their strength and their humility, never questioned the sanctity or the justness of their cause—the saving of pagan souls with the grace of Our Lord, Jesus Christ.

A *Missionary Album* in Honolulu contains this unexpectedly benign, and ultimately disregarded exhortation, to the First Company of missionaries:

> Your views are not to be limited to the low, narrow scale, but you are to open your hearts wide and set your goals high. You are to aim at nothing short of covering these islands with fruitful fields, and pleasant dwellings and schools and churches, and of raising up the whole people to an elevated state of Christian civilization. You are to obtain an adequate language of the people; to make them acquainted with letters, to give them the Bible, with skill to read it ... to introduce and get into extended operation and influence among them, the arts and institutions and usages of civilized life and society; and you are to abstain from all interference with local and political interests of the people and to inculcate the duties of justice, moderation, forbearance, truth and universal kindness. Do all in your power to make men of every class good, wise and happy.[2]

There were seven women in the First Company aboard the *Thaddeus* when it sailed from Boston in 1819. Five of the missionaries were ordained ministers; among the others were a printer, a physician, a bookbinder, a carpenter. Traveling with them were four young Hawaiian men—one of whom was called George Sandwich, perhaps in honor of the Islands, and another who was son to the King of Kaua'i—who had been students at the Cornwall Foreign Mission School in Connecticut. A pastor in Goshen, Connecticut, wrote in 1822 that one of the Hawaiian men, Hopu, had a "wicked disposition ... inclined rather to rove the sea."[3] During the War of 1812, however, this same man as a boy had been "shipwrecked about four hundred miles from the West Indies, [when] he rescued crew members from drowning by helping them get out of their clothes in the water.... Then he swam back to the wreck, tied a swamped boat to the mast, bailed it out and got the swimming crew aboard it. [The] next day he made a sail from the captain's 'frock' and navigated by the sun and stars six days to the West Indies, ... [where] the British ... relieved them of everything except the clothes they were wearing."[4] The roving Hopu later became a preacher in Kailua, his death occasioning the first missionary funeral in the Islands. One of the other Hawaiian boys educated in Connecticut became a schoolteacher, and another returned to the Islands to die drunk and dissolute. The young prince of Kaua'i, who married the daughter of the sailor Isaac Davis, disappointed the missionaries by reverting to bad habits and was captured in one of the few outbreaks of dissidence, "naked, foodless and drunk."[5]

The First Company landed on the arid west coast of the Big Island, making camp on a shadeless plain of black lava. They slept on mattresses balanced precariously on top of their trunks, taking refuge in frail huts made from branches gathered from the occasional coconut or *kou* tree. There was no fresh water; they became sick with flea bites. Refusing to bathe in the ocean, they were filthy as well as diseased. Lucia Holman, the wife of the physician, Dr. Thomas Holman, was horrified at the contemplation of a life "upon these barren rocks and among this heathen people, whose manners and habits are so rude and disgusting."[6] She unwisely admitted to her fellow traveler, the forbidding Lucy Thurston, that she "never would be willing to exercise that degree of self-denial which was called for by a situation among this people."[7] Mrs. Holman implored her husband to return to New England, but Dr. Holman removed his wife and himself to Honolulu instead, where he became physician to the king, a pleasant post for which he and his wife were better suited. In *Hawaii's Missionary Saga,* LaRue W. Piercy writes of the Holmans: "[They] were just basically of a different upbringing from the other missionaries in their company. Unlike the others, their marriage had not been one of emergency but of love and opportunity. Their inducement to missionary labors was the financial provision that solved their problems. They were bound not by an eager adventure in saving heathen souls but their personal longing for love and life."[8]

With the arrival of the missionaries, the astonished Hawaiians thought that children had been sent to them—when they heard English spoken they suspected it was *namu,* or gibberish. The more courageous among them ridiculed the foreigners, making obscene gestures and spying on them shamelessly when they were not poking and smelling them. Hundreds of natives, drawn by the odor of the strange food cooking on the lava flats, were confused by the eating habits of the foreigners. It was contrary to everything that they knew. The Hawaiians, given to feasting, had fed both themselves and their gods to bursting. Corpulence was a visible demonstration of wealth. This new god seemed to like his already slender followers to go hungry on his behalf. The missionaries were equally disconcerted by the diet of the Hawaiians, at first unaware that the shrill yelps coming from every gulch and cove signified the coming banquet for the first anniversary of Kamehameha's death. "Though often invited … to join them in partaking of the baked dog," writes Rev. William Ellis, "we were never induced to taste of one. The natives, however, say it is sweeter than the flesh of the pig, and much more palatable than that of goat or kids."[9]

Although the occasional nineteenth-century visitor found the natives to be industrious, civilized, and exceedingly polite, Rev. Hiram Bingham, ambitious leader of the First Company, perceived them in a state of "degradation, ignorance, pollution and destitution."[10] He was dismayed that Liholiho, given a Bible as a sign of the foreigners' friendly intentions, deigned to present himself without hat, gloves, shoes, stockings, or pants. The missionaries, ignorant that grave events had taken place only months before their arrival, did not know that upon the death of Kamehameha, Queen Ka'ahumanu had convinced Liholiho to abolish the old religion. Historical determinism aside, the Hawaiians grew to trust the foreigners in part because the missionaries had by chance fallen upon a dependent people only recently deprived of their gods. Soon enough, the Hawaiians carried fresh food and water to them in calabashes, and taught them to plant and harvest the strange crops of breadfruit, taro, and sugarcane. Liholiho's wife, Kamamalu, was moved to pity for the discommoded white ladies and had two large Chinese beds carried precipitously across the lava fields to them. Liholiho obligingly dispatched two of his men (one of them the historian John Papa Ii) to attend the new religion classes organized by the foreigners, and Queen Kamamalu, draped in seventy yards of an intricately patterned brown-and-white *pa'u* skirt made from the bark of the mulberry tree, cultivated an interest in the new faith. With the Hawaiian's disposition toward gaiety, his instinctive courtesy, his bewildered compliance taken, as is true with most colonized peoples, for weakness, he was seen as childlike and primitive—for the most part, although not entirely, innocent (the nakedness, the sensuality, the revelry). He was also thought to be in sore need of salvation.

One way to illumine myth is to question it. Bob Krauss, a popular contemporary columnist for the *Honolulu Advertiser,* has perfected the role of amiable iconoclast throughout his forty years of journalism. His columns were much admired in my childhood and frequently read aloud at the breakfast table to much surreptitious eye-rolling of the children. "An Italian sea captain landed in Hawaii with half a dozen of his crew. They intended to trade a bolt of bright red cloth for curios. On the beach they met a portly native queen flanked by an army of murderous-looking spearmen. She seized the cloth without even a thank you and ducked behind a bush. Faced with dozens of sharp-tipped spears, the Italian captain and his sailors could only shrug in resignation. A moment later, the queen emerged from behind the bush with the entire bolt of cloth wrapped around her. A leftover end was draped carelessly down one side. One of the crew members, who had been a tailor back in Italy, cried in disgust, 'That's-a-wrong, that's-a-wrong!'"[11]

Hiram Bingham, with the help of William Ellis, eventually became tutor to King Liholiho. Ellis, who seems to have had a sophistication not shared by his fellow Christians, grew fond of the young man. "His mind was naturally inquisitive," writes Ellis. "His general knowledge of the world was much greater than could have been expected. I have heard him entertain a party of chiefs for hours together, with accounts of different parts of the earth, describing the extensive lakes, the mountains, and mines of North and South America; the elephants and inhabitants of India.... He had a great thirst of knowledge ... [but] we do not know that Christianity exerted any decisive influence on his heart."[12]

The freedom that accompanied the emancipation from the ancient myths came with a terrible price. Not all the Hawaiians were as enthusiastic about the American missionaries as was Queen Kamamalu, but few understood that the abolition of the old rituals would inevitably render the culture weak and porous, ultimately leading to a collective loss of memory, if not annihilation. ("Religious ceremonies are, then," writes Eliade, "festivals of memory.")[13] With melancholy foresight, "some ... seemed to doubt the propriety of foreigners coming to reside permanently among them. They said they had heard that in several countries where foreigners had intermingled with the original natives, the latter had soon disappeared; and ... perhaps the land would ultimately become theirs, and the kanaka ... cease to be its occupiers."[14]

Ellis, despite his worldliness, was optimistic: "The population [of the Islands] at present is about 85,000 and will most probably be greatly increased by the establishment of Christianity, whose mild influence, it may reasonably be expected, will effect a cessation of war, an abolition of infanticide, and a diminution of those vices, principally of foreign origin, which have hitherto so materially contributed to the depopulation of the islands."[15] John Dominis Holt does not consider the role of missionary as conducive to morality or, for that matter, survival: "By thousands ... the Hawaiian began to disappear from the face of the earth. They willingly gave up their souls and died, or as it was said among themselves, *Na kanaka okuu wale aku no i kau uhane*, that is 'The people dismissed freely their souls and died.'"[15]

The population of Honolulu was between two and three thousand people at the time of the first missionaries. The town had grown into a convenient port for the ships embarking from the Pacific Northwest with their rich cargo of furs bound for the Chinese market, and the whaling ships from New England. An added mercantile inducement was the valuable Hawaiian sandalwood (soon depleted), carried to the harbor by long lines of naked natives. The small community consisted primarily of white men, and the strict rules soon put in place by the missionaries made for a sore curtailment of their pleasure as well as those of the Hawaiians. "Most of the foreigners in this place are decidedly opposed to the missionaries," writes Sarah Lyman twelve years after the arrival of the First Company.[17]

With the presence of the foreigner, whether sea captain or missionary, had come the use of alcohol. "Warmly disposed to the love of physical pleasure," writes Holt, "the enjoyment of which had been brought to great refinement in the old culture, the Hawaiians took to alcohol with a fatal and giddy determination."[18] Rev. Asa Thurston taught his Temperance Society to sing the following chant as they walked to service each Sunday from their homes in the mountains. The news that they hear refers to the gospel, preached by a Mr. Coan.

Mr. Thurston's Water-Drinking Brigade

Here's a song of the Water-Drinking Brigade,
brave warriors of Mr. Thurston's army.
Upstanding lads, girded well we journey forth
sparing no labor though weariness overtake.

Only late in the day do we hear the news,
golden news from the lowland:
Loud greetings to you, Mr. Coan,
preacher of the Word, salvation for the people![19]

So irresistible had the vice proved that during a tour of the world in 1881, the amiable King David Kalakaua had "disturbed the variety show at a public restaurant in the Prater [by howling fearfully], had taken off his uniform coat as soon as the dance began, had promiscuously kissed the women and, finally, the lackeys had to … [carry him] helplessly drunk, back to his hotel in the court-equipage…. The people … however, approved of the King's democratic manners, and when the band rendered the Hawaiian National Anthem, they rose and uncovered [their heads]."[20] As a girl, I was taught a song in Hawaiian called "Koni Au I Ka Wai" whose meaning I only learned years later: "I throb, I throb for liquid, I throb for cool liquid, royal liquid—gin—to make life cool and peaceful."[21]

Despite the dislike of the white businessmen and seamen, as well as some of the Hawaiians, the missionaries, as is the nature of missionaries, were undaunted. They at once learned to speak Hawaiian in order to preach to the natives in their own very poetic language, bestowing upon them an alphabet of twelve letters (a, e, h, i, k, l, m, n, o, p, u, w). "Commenced reading chemistry to-day with the design of devoting one hour in the day to it, as a sort of relaxation from the language,"[22] writes Sarah Lyman soon after her arrival. The Hawaiian language is not difficult to learn, given that all vowels are sounded, although not necessarily enunciated. For example, Waikiki is pronounced Why-kee-KEE, eliding the *a* and the first *i*. Lai'e, however, is pronounced La-EE-a. The *w* before the last letter in a word is always pronounced *v* (although until the middle of the nineteenth century, the letter *k* was pronounced *t* as in Tamehameha, and *l* was pronounced *r*). The difference between a long and short vowel is negligible. Every syllable ends with a vowel; the accent is almost always on the penultimate syllable. Most words, however, can be adverbs, adjectives, nouns, or verbs; the meaning of a sentence determined by the placement of a word and its accompanying particles.

When the native women first watched the missionary ladies make clothes on a sewing machine, the word *holoku* (a graceful, fitted long dress often with a little train) was contrived; the word *holo* (to run) combined with *ku* (standing erect) to describe the stitches of the wondrous machine. Sometimes new words were fashioned by giving a Hawaiian spelling to an English word; *Mele Kalikimaka* for "Merry Christmas." As there is no *s* in Hawaiian, my name is rendered Kukana. *Pikake*, the jasmine flower, is the Hawaiian word for "peacock"—the Princess Kai'ulani kept peacocks at her estate, 'Ainahau. A new word was often created through misunderstanding. As a ship is called *moku*, island, because of the belief that Captain Cook traveled on a floating island, steamships were later called *mokuahi*, floating fire-islands. *Pake*, still a derogatory term for a Chinese, is a mis-use of the Chinese word for "Honorable Brother." *Popoki*, cat, is said to be a mispronunciation of "poor pussy."

The missionaries cannot have been fully aware of the symbolism in the Hawaiian language, given their triumph in maintaining a willful ignorance as well as a genuine innocence.

FROM THE COLLECTION OF RICK AND QUACK MOORE

19th century: A woman wearing a pa'u *skirt*

The word for a beloved person is literally translated, "a flower not spread." To be aloof or aristocratic, *paliloa,* is to be "a tall and distant cliff." A much loved child is "a spring that goes on and on." In truth, there are very few words capable of expressing abstraction—it would be impossible to begin this sentence with the words, "In truth." The language assigns a different name to each night of the moon, the phases of the moon intimately connected to planting and fishing as well as to making love. Admiration is evoked for the Inuit and his numerous words for snow, but surely other languages have a similar abundant specificity—the Hawaiians possess endless words for the ocean; endless words for the changing sky; endless words for the many kinds of rain.

The Irish poet Padraic Colum was given a grant in the 1930s by the Territorial Legislature of Hawai'i to gather an anthology of Hawaiian poetry. "The penchant for kaona or indirection is only partially explicable by the vagueness of the language occasioned in some parts by lack of sexual gender, verbs without subjects or objects, and verbless sentences," writes Samuel H. Elbert of Colum's effort. "[Colum] rewrote them in an Irish vein. He did not know the language, but saw hidden meanings everywhere, and he claimed that every Hawaiian Poem had at least four meanings—an ostensible meaning, a vulgar meaning, a mythico-historical-topographical meaning, and a deeply hidden meaning.... To say that every poem has a vulgar meaning sounds like a comment by some of the more extreme nineteenth-century missionaries."[23] To be fair to Colum, a song about the first automobile in a collection by Elbert and Noelani Mahoe is translated: "I worry about the clanking sound, Springs broken top to bottom, Passion calmed, So delightful."[24]

The missionaries also gave to the people a regional costume. The women were quickly enveloped in long loose smocks with high yoked neck and long sleeves called a Mother Hubbard, later to be called a *mu'umu'u,* which must have made swimming a bit cumbersome, as well as exaggerating the natural restrictions of climate and landscape. Mrs. Katherine Gerould, traveling in the Islands nearly a century ago, could not have been more delighted at the adaptation. She writes in *Hawaii Scenes and Impressions:* "Tradition says that the first missionary ladies, in mad haste to dress their converts, handed over the patterns of their own nightgowns. A race (I submit) that has stuck faithfully for nearly a hundred years to the model of our great-grandmothers' nightdresses ... is a docile, an admirable, a lovable race."[25]

Despite these questionable gifts, the missionaries, as is the nature of missionaries, were there to take things away. Both the healthful and less salutary diversions of generations, which the missionaries equated with pagan religious practice and insidious secular pleasure, were declared sinful and replaced by segregated classes in needlework, theology, and English grammar. The chants and hula, most of which had been passed from generation to generation for centuries, were forbidden; a suppression that would prove catastrophic for the Hawaiians. The chants contained everything a person needed to know about the world; it was a way to worship the gods, to call warriors to battle, to mourn a king, to court a lover, to celebrate the birth of a child. Each successive generation, listening and memorizing

LYMAN MUSEUM, HARRY A. WESSEL COLLECTION

Hilo, 19th century: Haole man with Hawaiian woman in the Mother Hubbard dress created by the missionaries for native women.

the stories told to it, inevitably altered the chants and meles in the retelling. Because of this constant modification and embellishment, the myths were not required to be consistent or accurate, particularly in regard to dates or facts, which license only added to the missionaries' disdain.

The chanting of the myths constituted the core of an oral tradition representing far more than an interest in music or history. Place-names as well as personal names were didactic of both history and geography, formally binding the bearer to a physical as well as to a spiritual past. The long genealogies, traditionally composed with the pregnancy of a princess, linked the high chiefs "not only to the primary gods belonging to the whole people and worshipped in common with allied Polynesian groups," writes Martha Beckwith, "not only to deified chiefs born into the living world ... but to the stars in the heavens and the plants and animals useful to life on earth."[26] An irreplaceable loss of meaning occurs as myth is abandoned. The practice of remembering itself suffers.

Sports and games were also proscribed by the missionaries. "As the legitimate consequences of their servile and wretched condition, females of every unevangelized land are devoid of those sentiments of delicacy, and that refined taste and acute discrimination between the lovely and the disgusting in manners and customs," writes Caleb Wright, "which distinguish ... the sex in lands unenlightened by the gospel. Before Christianity commenced its reign in the Society Islands, wrestling was a favourite pastime of females."[27] Surf-riding, practiced by both sexes, usually nude, was forbidden. Gambling, of which the Hawaiians were inordinately fond, was prohibited. "We have seen females hazarding their beads, scissors, cloth-beating mallets, and every piece of cloth they possessed, except what they wore, on a throw," writes Rev. William Ellis.[28] Even the children were pressed to give up their pets—this song was taught to the tune of Yankee Doodle Dandy:

Don't beat my dog,
My pretty dog,
Friend to go with, friend to sleep with,
Friend to play with.

Drive away your dog,
Says the wise one.
Fleas, bites, mean,
Noisy, naughty.

His bark bow wow
So noisy.
Steals, wastes money,
Eats the house's wealth.

Kill
Your "pretty dog,"
Save money, buy books,
Wealth for heaven. [29]

The missionaries tried to counter the belief in *'aumakuas,* or totems, but they were not able to completely eradicate this vestige of the old religion. Every Hawaiian family possessed its own 'aumakua that served as helper and protector (an 'aumakua might be an owl, a cowrie, an eel, or a limpet, among other things), a custom which continues to this day. The missionaries also failed to suppress the old practice of praying someone to death, *ana'ana,* which was often commissioned by an envious acquaintance. Fortunately, a friend of the victim, or the victim if quick enough, could in turn ask the sorcerer to reverse the spell so that it would fly back to the murderer and kill him in revenge: "Death in the heavens; corruption in the heavens; maggots in the heavens; mildew in the heavens. Heaven speed the death of ana'ana." An alarming tradition, impervious to repression, it was still possible in the 1970s for physicians in Hawai'i to be asked to treat patients under a bewitchment or death-prayer. "*I ka olelo no ke ola, I ka olelo no ka make.* In the word is life, in the word is death."

CHAPTER SEVEN

The Islands

If we take for myth an explanation of the natural world and how it came into being, then it was the beneficent rain god, Lono, who brought the first cultivated plants to the Hawaiian Islands. Less poetically, life came to the Islands "via wind, water, or wing."[1] A seed washed ashore with the high tide of a storm or in the flotsam of a shipwreck, or fell from the feathers or droppings of a bird blown from its normal migration. "Indeed it is hypothesized that such an event occurred nearly 300 times during the history of the archipelago," writes botanists Robert Gustafson and S. H. Sohmer. "Flora had been derived over time via the establishment of 272 successful introductions. Dividing this number into the number of years available in which such natural introductions could have occurred ... leads to the conclusion that, on average, one successful introduction need have occurred once every 20,000-30,000 years.... If one takes 70 million years as the life of the entire archipelago from Hawai'i Island to the Aleutian Trench [encompassing numerous islands such as Laysan, Necker, Brooks Shoal, and Hermes Reef], such an event need not have occurred more than once every 250,000 years."[2]

The god Lono did it in far less time, even if Hawai'i, the largest island although the youngest in geological age, possessed vast tracts of barren lava where it was exceedingly difficult to cultivate life. On the other islands, the topography is less harsh; in all the islands there is endless sunshine, and there is abundant rainfall—the northeast trade wind, flowing at less than ten thousand feet, creates a wave of wind that moves across the sea heavy with moisture.[3] Each of the Islands is surrounded by a narrow hem of shallow water, and the steep underwater drop allows for abundant and easy fishing.

The first settlers known to reach the Hawaiian Islands were Polynesians, not more than several hundred, who sailed in big ocean canoes from the Marquesas in the South Pacific around A.D. 600. It is not known for certain why they undertook their long and hazardous sea journey. Perhaps they were castaways, or refugees from a war, or survivors of a royal dynastic struggle, or victims of a famine. There may have been a myth of a chain of mountainous islands to the northeast; they may just have been curious wanderers. Whatever the reason for their journey, they were greatly aided by the natural currents and winds of the Pacific. A Maori navigator and steersman of canoes in the Cook Islands once told me that he knew everything—the temperature, the direction of the wind, the direction of the current, the distance from landfall, the depth of the water—simply by putting his hand into the water.

The travelers brought thirty species of plants with them, including the yam, breadfruit and taro, the mulberry, and plants for healing and for sorcery. They carried jungle fowl and pigs, dogs, and, presumably unintentionally, the rat. Ferns and the pandanus *(hala)* provided the only plant food growing in the Hawaiian Islands when they landed, with birds (some of them flightless as they had no natural enemies until the arrival of the Marquesans with their animals) and bats for food. Crops of taro, sweet potato, sugar, and arrowroot were soon grown, as well as other roots and trees.

Although anthropologists bemoan the early history of the Islands as imprecise, thanks to an oral tradition and a preponderance of myth, there is sufficient evidence to suggest that the first Polynesian settlers were soon organized into productive communities with chiefs, nobility, priests, commoners, and slaves. Despite the limitation of a primitive digging stick, which they did not trouble to modify over the centuries (as the American Indian did not make the wheel), the Hawaiians developed an effective system of agriculture, and a thorough knowledge of engineering,[4] even if the Menehune, the tiny aborigines who were said to have fled to the mountains with the arrival of the tall strangers from the Marquesas, crept from their hiding places at night to plant the crops and dig the canals for irrigation.

At the time of Cook's arrival, there were approximately 1,300 species of flowering plants, 90 percent of which could not be found anywhere else in the world. The English captain, George Vancouver, who first saw Hawai'i as Cook's midshipman in 1778, later spent several tranquil months in the Islands from

1792 to 1794 on his journey to complete the survey of the northwest American coast left unfinished with Cook's death. Well-received by Kamehameha I and his prime minister, John Young, Vancouver was the first traveler to note in detail the restive volcanoes of the Big Island: "Several columns of smoke were seen to descend which Tameameah and the rest of our friends said were occasioned by the subterranean fires that frequently broke out in violent eruptions."[5] The Hawaiian scholar, Mary Kawena Pukui, translates a chant composed by the goddess Hiʻiaka, younger sister of the fire goddess Pele, praising Pele's own district of Hilo, the home of my brothers and sister-in-law.

Hiʻiaka's Song at Panaʻewa

*I lose my breath crossing Hilo region's rivers and
    ravines,
countless hills, descents innumerable as I travel
Kulaʻimano's gullies and streams....*

*Panaʻewa the rain-drenched forest-island of tallest
    trees,
dense branches of scraggly lehua,
ʻohiʻa's flame-flower, beloved of forest birds.*

*Now Hilo darkens. Night falls in Hilo.
Puna, sunk in dusk, glows through my smoky land.
All things stir with life, breathe anew.*

The Woman has lighted her fires.[6]

The amiable Captain Vancouver brought sheep and goats to the Hawaiian Islands, as well as orange seedlings from the Society Islands. He was to be responsible, however, for the destruction of much of Hawai'i's indigenous and endemic plant life as well as some of its birds, thanks to the introduction of cattle from California. The "young bull calf nearly full grown, two fine cows, and two very fine bull calves, all in high condition"[7] brought by Vancouver bred so rapidly that, twenty years later, Rev. William Ellis saw enormous herds of them ranging destructively over the hillsides. The cattle and horses also destroyed the houses of the natives by eating the thatch.

By the middle of the century, the residents of the Islands who took an interest in natural history, as well as those amateur and professional scientists who studied the biota of the archipelago, were well aware of the fast deterioration of native flora and fauna. In an article on land shells written in 1856 for the *Sandwich Islands Monthly Magazine,* the writer noted that "the numerous herd of wild cattle rushing with their extended horns through the forests ... nearly extinguished many fine species that we had formerly found in abundance."[8] E. Alison Kay, a malacologist at the University of Hawaii, quotes Mrs. F. Sinclair, writing in 1885: "The Hawaiian flora seems (like the native human inhabitant) to grow in an easy, careless way, which, though pleasingly artistic, and well adapted to what may be termed the natural state of the islands, will not long survive the invasions of foreign plants and changed conditions. Forest fires, animals and agriculture, have so changed the islands, within the last fifty or sixty years, that one can now travel for miles, in some districts, without finding a single

LYMAN MUSEUM, HARRY A. WESSEL COLLECTION

Hilo Bay, 19th century: The lady is holding fruit of the hala, *or* pandanus, *tree.*

indigenous plant; the ground being wholly taken possession of by weeds, shrubs, and grasses, imported from various countries. It is remarkable that plants from both tropical and temperate regions seem to thrive equally well on these islands, many of them spreading as if by magic, and rapidly exterminating much of the native flora."[9]

The pig and the rat brought by the first Polynesian settlers had proved very destructive (Boswell's guidebook points out that there are no snakes in Hawai'i: "Circus snakes are placed under special guard until they leave the Islands.")[10] The rat alone devoured many of the fifty species of flightless birds that have been identified only through the discovery of their fossils.

One early explorer, failing in his ascent of Mauna Loa, wrote, "After leaving the breadfruit forests we continued ... to the distance of a mile and an half further, and found the land thick covered with wild fern.... We found the country here as well as the sea shore universally overspread with lava, and also saw several subterranean excavations that had every appearance of past eruption and fire.... We had also shot a number of fine birds of the liveliest and most variegated plumage that any of us had ever met with, but we heard no melody among them."[11] Perhaps the birds were silent because they knew their fate: the o'o, last seen in 1837; the *kioea*, last seen in 1859; the greater koa finch, last seen in 1896; the *ula-ai-hawane*, last seen in the early 1890s; the black mamo, last seen in 1907; the Laysan honeycreeper, last seen in 1923.

In the list of newly extinct species that is published each year in the *New York Times*, Hawai'i possesses the most losses of any state by a large number. The *Times* reported on November 25, 2002, that wildlife officials hope to capture the last three *po'ouli* birds in the world, said to be the rarest birds on Earth, living within a mile and a half of each other in a Maui rain forest (ornithologists believe that the three birds have never seen one another). As a girl I kept a melancholy notebook of the flora and fauna that had disappeared in the Hawaiian Islands, among them the *'ahinahina*, the silversword, the lovely spiderflower, and two species of *Phyllostegia*.

Not so long ago, a friend sitting on the beach at her family's house in Malaekahana on the north shore of O'ahu happened to notice a turtle, the size and shape of a quarter, staggering across the sand to the sea. The turtle, after many cumbersome attempts, at last tumbled into the surf where, to my friend's dismay, it began to drown. She dashed into the water to save it. After some trouble, she found it, but the turtle was not strong enough to swim despite being ferried beyond the breaking surf to deep water, and she reluctantly carried it back to shore. She filled a bucket with seawater and went to the Kahuku market, the old company store where the indebted Chinese and Japanese workers once forfeited their meager weekly wages for scrip (as opposed to cash-money), and she bought raw shrimp, which she chopped into minuscule pieces to feed the turtle. After a few days, when it grew apparent that the turtle was dying, she called the oceanographic institute to inquire if she should alter the turtle's diet or the temperature of the water. She was startled to learn upon describing the turtle that she had rescued a species last seen in 1943, so rare as to be thought extinct. Her picture, with the turtle balanced on the tip of her finger, was on the front page of the newspaper and she was given a lifetime pass to the institute, which promptly confiscated the turtle.

CHAPTER EIGHT

The Collectors

The earliest drawings of the Hawaiian Islands were made either by professional artists accompanying a formal expedition or, less frequently, by the occasional traveler given to sketching. "During the twelve years from 1768 to 1780," writes Bernard Smith, "something in the order of three thousand original drawings were made of things, mostly from the Pacific, not seen before by Europeans: plants, fish, molluscs, birds, coastlines, landscapes, unknown peoples, their arts and crafts, religious practices and styles of life.... Cook's voyages were not only fact-gathering phenomena, they deeply affected conceptual thought, and their influence penetrated deeply into the aesthetic realm."[1]

These renderings were to be instrumental in the provocation of the Western imagination, and in the creation of new myths.

It is thanks to men such as William Ellis (not the English missionary), Cook's official artist aboard the *Resolution,* and Robert Dampier that we possess an unsentimental record of eighteenth- and early nineteenth-century Hawai'i and its people.

Robert Dampier, an Englishman born in Wiltshire, was taken on board the H.M.S. *Blonde* (whose captain was Byron's cousin) in Rio de Janeiro in 1824 as official artist during the ship's melancholy journey to the Islands with the bodies of King Liholiho and Queen Kamamalu, who had died suddenly of measles on a visit to London. On Dampier's arrival in the new town of Honolulu, he requested of the aging regent, Ka'ahumanu, permission to paint the royal family, enticing her with the promise that he wished to show the portraits to the English king, George IV.[2]

In these early paintings and descriptions of Hawai'i, we glimpse a people caught mid-stride between two worlds— a man wearing a linen waistcoat, beaver hat, and no trousers; a young chief smoking a pipe crudely fashioned from a twisted tree branch; a dancer tattooed across her body with the traditional aniconic symbols of Polynesia with the addition of a few scampering English goats encircling her bare breasts. To Dampier's dismay, the chiefs and chiefesses insisted on being painted in the serge and cotton they had recently acquired. He much preferred his sitters in native dress. One of his subjects, the young princess Nahi'ena'ena, was a daughter of Kamehameha I and his highest ranking wife, Keopuolani. She wears the traditional red and yellow feather capelet of the ali'i in her portrait, artfully arranged by Dampier to conceal her black silk dress. Dampier writes that the old queen regent, furious that the artist had begun the portrait of the princess before her own sitting, "stalked into the room full dressed, demanding that I should leave off the one I had already commenced."[3] It was not until he had finished painting Ka'ahumanu (the portrait has since disappeared) that Dampier was allowed to finished the portrait of Nahi'ena'ena. The princess, under the proud guardianship of Mr. and Mrs. Steward in Lahaina, was held in great esteem by those who converted her to Christianity. In a profound confusion, she suffered a nervous collapse and was dead at twenty-two.[4]

Hawaiian nobility had already given up the silk cloaks called *kihei* that the chiefesses had traditionally worn thrown over the left shoulder, leaving the right arm free and the right breast exposed, the form of drapery also affected by Amazon warriors who were thought to cut off a breast so as to more comfortably shoot an arrow. "Both sexes are uncommonly fond of ornamenting their persons," Dampier writes, "and evince a great deal of taste in forming chaplets of flowers and wreaths for their heads and necks.... These they arrange upon their heads in the most tasteful manner."[5] Ten years after Dampier made his lovely paintings, Sarah Lyman reminds us in her letters that missionaries have a marked effect on aesthetics as well as morals: "It is the custom to ornament their heads with garlands of bright red and yellow flowers made with a great deal of labor but which fade in a day or two, and also to wear ... strings of bright yellow beads ... which have a very disagreeable smell.... I soon made them tabu in my school and have always used my influence to put them down."[6] Forty years later, the impact of the missionaries had been somewhat ameliorated and beauty was again in favor. The Englishwoman Isabella Bird, sent around the world by her doctor to alleviate a propensity to depression, discovered herself to be not only highly intelligent, but unusually venturesome (and not so depressed). She wrote books about Hawai'i, Persia, Korea, and China, as well as Japan and the Rocky Mountains of Canada. Bird found the Hawaiian women enchanting, particularly in comparison to their white sisters: "They ... are free from our tasteless perversity as to colour and ornament, and have an instinct of the becoming.... A majestic wahine with small, bare feet, a grand, swinging, deliberate gait, hibiscus blossoms in her flowing hair, and a lei of yellow flowers following over her holoku, marching through these streets, has a tragic grandeur of appearance, which makes the diminutive, fair-skinned haole, tottering along hesitatingly in high-heeled shoes, look grotesque by comparison."[7]

Robert Dampier managed to make a series of five portraits of the ali'i and a portfolio of landscape sketches that were later reproduced in his memoir of his journey (he contributed to the myth by putting fanciful palm trees in his landscapes). He also wrote one of the first descriptions of Honolulu, then pronounced Hon-o-RU-ru, spreading haphazardly on either side of Nu'uanu Stream. From the extinct volcano known as Punchbowl Hill to the Americans (and Hill of Sacrifice to the Hawaiians), Dampier describes the town: "The habitations, with the exception of a few houses ... are all built with straw. ... Very little attention has been paid in forming this cluster of huts into anything like a town or Village: here and there ... sufficient regularity has been observed to form a street or two....

COLLECTION OF RICK AND QUACK MOORE

Late 19th century: Hula girls

There are four or five decent houses erected by the Americans, one or two of stone, the others of wood."[8] The town seemed little influenced by Western design, even if its existence was dependent upon the foreigners. All the same, some advances had been made. In 1806, a shipwrecked Japanese fisherman had dismissively described Honolulu as a place without mosquitoes or wedding ceremonies.[9]

Hawai'i, already fixing itself at the start of the nineteenth century in the imagination of the West as a place of piquant palms and lissome naked women in flower wreaths, was not, however, a source of artistic stimulation for the Protestant missionaries who began to arrive in 1820. These earnest, sometimes hard-done-by souls did not pause to make drawings of their new home other than the hurried renderings tucked into the letters sent East to concerned friends and relatives; but even had they found the time to paint, it was not their inclination. This is not to say that they did not see the extraordinary beauty of their new island home despite their prurient alarm and domestic discomfort, but that the missionaries had not come all that distance, undertaking a dangerous sea journey, forsaking comfortable New England parsonages and farmhouses, for the views. Young Mrs. Loomis of the First Company innocently let slip her surprising fascination with the hula, and some of the missionaries were to collect chants and songs, but only in the interest of liturgical transposition. There was little time for such indulgences as painting, even were it not dangerous to look.

Fortunately, others were looking. "The history of the visual arts in Europe [since] 1750 ... can best be understood as the steady, relentless and continuing triumph of empirical naturalism over classical naturalism. And at the starting point of that triumph," writes Bernard Smith, "there is no single more significant factor to be found than the graphic-arts programme that was developed in the course of Captain Cook's three voyages and the discussions that attended the publications of its results."[10]

The interest in the natural history of Polynesia increased in proportion to the decline of voyages of exploration. The Islands were visited by the ships of Prussia, Great Britain, Denmark, France, Russia, and the United States, bringing with them all types and temperaments of men, some of them amateurs eager for rare souvenirs (seashells were carried surreptitiously to London by sailors bribed by dealers frantic to satisfy their customers' avidity for a cabinet of curiosities)[11] and some of them trained scientists. They came to paint flowers, measure trees, take readings of the barometer, survey the land, label birds and insects, estimate heights and temperatures; they were pharmacists, draughtsmen, surveyors, portrait painters, engineers, sea captains, surgeons. The collectors, earnest if not always rigorous, sometimes suffered the unfortunate mishap: "A variety of hazards were reflected in the fate of the collections ... [the] complaint that the 'vile cockroaches ate up all of the Paper' on which ... astronomical observations were recorded was perhaps not unexpected in the tropics," writes E. Alison Kay. "Other events were not anticipated: many of the collections of the United States Exploratory Expedition were lost in the wreck of the *Peacock,* as were eighteen cases of collections of the *Uranie* when she was wrecked near Cape Horn. Several collections were mixed during the course of long voyages that touched at many ports, or in the workrooms of the closet naturalists who described the specimens, leading to mistakes in classification and attribution."[12] One of the more competent scientists was the Scottish botanist David Douglas (for whom the fir is named) who stayed with Rev. David and Mrs. Lyman in Hilo in 1834. Until his mysterious death in a Big Island cattle pit that year, Douglas sent hundreds of plants from Oʻahu and Hawaiʻi to Sir Joseph Hooker at Kew Gardens, as well as a pair of nene geese that miraculously survived the journey. So keen was the new passion for natural history that a small room at the Seamen's Bethel in Honolulu was hastily set up as a makeshift museum containing "a few shells & minerals, a large black bear, a very few native weapons, poor Douglas' snowshoes, etc."[13]

Despite themselves, the missionaries and in particular their children proved invaluable collectors in the end. On leaving the Islands for college, the second and third generations of mission families "took with them their natural history collections: skulls, shells, birds and plants. 'That box of skulls was a lucky thing for me,' wrote Sanford B. Dole to his father, 'especially in introducing me among the scientific men of Boston.' The 'scientific men' included Dana, Asa Gray, and Louis Agassiz.... As remarkable as the interest and productivity of the missionary resident naturalists is the reflection in their work ... of the changing philosophy of science in the nineteenth century. In the 1820s, as S. E. Bishop described it, 'Of geology we never heard. The globe had been created in six ordinary days, and there was no mystery about it.' ... Within thirty years, John T. Gulick was writing, 'These *Achatinellinae* never came from Noah's ark.'"[14]

CHAPTER NINE

The Missionary

Sarah Joiner, daughter of Salmon Joiner and Mary Moore, born in an isolated village in Vermont, traveled in 1830 to Boston where she attended the meetings of the American Board of Commissioners for the Missions, finding time to hear a lecture by the famous Dr. Beecher. Perhaps stimulated by meeting Henry Lyman, a young gentleman from the Andover Theological Seminary (later killed by natives in Sumatra while exercising his faith), she wrote in her diary the reasons she was not fit for recruitment in God's elect army: "In the first place I have not been so decidedly pious as I ought, my influence has not been exerted in favour of religion, and if I neglect to improve upon the opportunities of doing good among my kindred and acquaintance, surely I am not a fit person to go on a mission.... I have not strong nerves, and this is certainly what a missionary ought to have."[1]

Ten months later, the twenty-six-year-old Sarah was putting her nerves to the test as she traveled by ship to the Sandwich Islands with a relative of Henry Lyman, her new husband, Rev. David Belden Lyman of New Hartford, Connecticut. Like many of the missionary wives who married straight from the schoolroom thanks to the efficient connivance of the theological seminaries, Sarah Lyman had known her life's companion but a few weeks' time before consenting to accompany him on a dangerous journey halfway across the world to a land of heathens.

The new Mrs. Lyman, that summer of 1832, looked first upon the broad and sloping flank of Mauna Loa as they came upon the islands from the east. The crest of the mountain was covered, surprisingly, in snow; the verdant hillsides planted with bananas and cane. The leeward slopes, devoid of plantation, were thick with tall *pili* grass; the barren plains of lava descended in long plateaus to beaches of black volcanic sand. Mrs. Lyman thanked her Redeemer: "A kind Providence [that] has protected us and led us on our way when dangers have stood thick around, and ... brought us after eight months of wandering to the field where we trust it is His will we should labour."[2]

The missionaries had been at work in the Islands for twelve years and Mrs. Lyman was not prepared to find the native people so abject. She was shocked. "Poor creatures how I pity them as I see them almost entirely destitute of clothing, all the sympathies of my soul are awakened to them. I earnestly desire to have it in my power to do them good.... I had not correct ideas of their condition. The majority of them are more filthy than the swine. Their houses are wretched hovels, and the abode of vermin, and the inhabitants covered with sores from head to foot. Some are afflicted with boils, some with sore eyes and a variety of diseases unheard in our country, arising no doubt from a want of cleanliness. But the awful stupidity which every where prevails among the people, is enough to call forth the sympathies and prayers of all who have an interest at the throne of grace."[3] She writes in June of the death in Honolulu of the queen who had abolished the gods. Ka'ahumanu, called the "reformer of her nation" by the missionaries, was one of the last links to the ancient world, if only because she had initiated its demise. "I heard lamentations and weeping among the natives.... Kaahumanu was dead.... Multitudes of natives were running to and fro.... We were appraised of the near approach of the body of the queen by the beating of drums.... The corpse was carried on the shoulders of several of the natives, covered with a black pall. The young king and Mr. Bingham rode on horseback just before it. The chiefs were scattered among the crowd. A vast number of natives followed in trains, uttering the most bitter lamentations. The king and the chiefs were silent."[4]

Arriving on the Big Island, Rev. David and Mrs. Lyman spent their first night as guests of the old king's counselor, John Young. They traveled across the mountains from Kona to their post in the village of Hilo in a driving rain that was to last a fortnight. Hilo, a muddy village on the slopes of Mauna Loa without roads or wooden dwellings, had been established as a mission in 1824, a year before the artist Robert Dampier's arrival in the Islands. Dampier made several drawings and descriptions of Hilo: "On all sides the most lively verdure prevails, luxuriant breadfruit trees flourish to the water's edge; these are thickly intermingled with towering cocoanut trees; amongst these are scattered the neat looking huts of the natives. In the distance the gigantic forms of Mowna Kaah [Mauna Kea] & Mowna Roa [Mauna Loa], rear their towering crests to the clouds."[5] Despite Dampier's admiration, Sarah Lyman was not taken with the views, nor did she find the manners of the natives pleasing: "Both men and women, if they have occasion for it will sit down in, or by the side of the road to do their duties, right before our eyes too.... I am often put to the blush."[6] She at once began a school, enlisting a hundred native girls dressed in gowns of black tapa cloth, straw hats, and leis. Among her classes were chemistry, map drawing, and arithmetic. For the three months it took to build their own house, she and her husband lived in a traditional native hut of thatch that, surprisingly, she found to be peaceful in a place that was stranger and wilder than she could have imagined during Dr. Beecher's lecture. If she was dismayed by the filth, she was made desperate by the immorality, undoubtedly seeing a connection between the two vices. She suffered over the lax morals of the Hawaiians, fretting that surfing, among other odious pastimes, led to "intercourse with the sexes without discrimination."[7] She seemed justified in her anxiety when a native drowned while surfing, and naively hoped that it would at last prove a lesson to the people. The Hawaiians under her care were confused by the new missionaries' litany of rules, and the young students at the Lymans' boarding school were intimidated. "One of our most intelligent young men came to me last night to know if it would be right for him to procure water to drink,"[8] writes Mrs. Lyman in admiration. The Hawaiian children also proved difficult as boarders due to their inordinate fear of ghosts, among them the night marchers.

Despite her repugnance, Sarah Lyman could not help but recognize that the Hawaiian race was disappearing. "When these islands were discovered they were teeming with inhabitants.... [I]n 1821 ... [there were] 80,000 inhabitants on this island [of Hawai'i]; in 1827 there was but 50,000. [Since 1836] ... they have diminished one tenth. If they shall continue to diminish in that ratio for a few years to come they will become extinct."[9] If it occurs to Mrs. Lyman that she and her fellow evangelists have advanced this decimation, she does not say so. The missionaries were not coldhearted; they felt a distinct concern that was a mixture of disapproval, pity, and a sense of Christian duty. In time, some of them even came to love the people. Despite her ambivalence and years of fragile health in part brought on by hard work, Sarah Lyman at the end of her long life (she died in Hilo in 1885) considered her husband's mission a triumph, and so it was. Writing fifty years after her arrival, working on her myth, she describes the Hawaiians quite differently than she had in the 1830s: "The people were numerous and had a healthy look; they were docile and very friendly. Nearly all were clad in their native costume ... those were halcyon days, when we were permitted to do the work for which we came ... and they are now remembered with unfeigned pleasure."[10]

I was to contribute to the myth 150 years later in a novel, *Sleeping Beauties.* Mabel Wilcox, the youngest child of Sarah Lyman's youngest child, is one of the models for the character named Emma. Miss Mabel, who lived at Grove Farm on Kaua'i, was a plump spinster given to sensible white lace-up shoes and patterned cotton frocks. Like some of her ancestors, she was disposed to good works. She had a fondness for See's Chocolates which were sent to her from Honolulu. In the novel, the character Miss Emma is sophisticated (she listens to John Coltrane records), but under no circumstances could Mabel Wilcox ever have been called worldly. "Emma, who was the granddaughter of Princess Ruth, had inherited Wisteria House," I wrote in 1993:

> Clio [Emma's young niece] used to imagine that nothing had come off the ships in Honolulu harbor that did not pass through the rooms of Wisteria House: the first grand piano ever seen in the islands, the first refrigerator, the first carriage and pair, the first Brazil nut. By the time Clio arrived at Wisteria House, faded red and yellow capes from the time of Kamehameha I, woven from the breast feathers of thousands of little birds, lay stiffly over dusty koa tables.... Carved idols with abalone-shell eyes and mouths of sharks' teeth leaned disconsolately against the walls, their upraised arms bound in clotted webs, their shoulders powdered with the dried wings of bats and birds.... The treasure and detritus of six generations of collectors filled the house, the possessions not of scholars or antiquaries, but of ordinary people who simply could not throw away anything: quilts, hymnals, the weightless

skulls of owls, netted calabashes, chipped Venetian glass, koa bedsteads, makaloa mats, paintings on black velvet, crates of China tea, jawbone fish hooks, ukiyo-e, bolts of silk, stovepipe hats, lauhala sails, pink crepe gowns from Callot Soeurs, polo mallets, one stuffed nene goose, and every proclamation of Queen Lili'uokalani's court from 1891 to the day of her bitter abdication.

CHAPTER TEN

The Gentry

"So well did they [the missionaries] succeed in this, and also in civilizing the kanaka," wrote Jack London at the start of the twentieth century, "that by the second or third generation he was practically extinct.... This being the fruit of the seed of the Gospel, the fruit of the seed of the missionaries (the sons of the grandsons) was the possession of the islands themselves, of the land, the ports, the town-sites and the sugar plantations."[1]

In 1848, when King Kamehameha III issued the Great Mahele in the hope of more equitably sharing the land, the large estates given to the missionaries promptly were made into sugar plantations and cattle ranches. Given the belief in the natural indolence of the native, foreign indentured labor—initially from China and later from Japan (the first thousand contract laborers from Japan arrived in 1885, and by 1907 constituted the largest ethnic group in the Islands), Spain (1898), Puerto Rico (1900), and the Philippines (1907)—was swiftly imported, put into workers' camps, and sent to work in the fields.

Sarah Lyman writes of the indentured servants brought from China to work on the new plantations, quite a few of which were owned by her children and friends: "Whilst I am writing I hear them singing at their work, which I think they like better than washing, for several of them have tried at that and they neither seem to know anything about that, or like it."[2] By this time, Mrs. Lyman found the Hawaiians to be far more civilized than the Orientals—the very appearance of the Chinese was less pleasing than that of the natives. In 1866, however, her son, Rufus Lyman, was to marry Miss Rebecca Hualani Brickwood, daughter of one Louise Chu Chu Gilman and her husband, the rich Chinese merchant, Ahung. (In a book published in 1916, Mrs. Gerould writes, "The Chinaman, ploughing his rice-fields with the classic water-buffalo, sitting decorously in his tidy shop, or selling unspeakable foods in his markets, lends a grave and welcome note to the medley.")[3] Sarah Lyman describes the Chinese cemetery in Manoa Valley in 1851: "The boys at Punahou go out to witness the ceremonies and are treated with cakes and after the Chinamen have left, they gather up what they can find."[4] A hundred years later, I, too, was a student at Punahou, the preparatory school founded for the children of the missionaries in 1841. After my mother died when I was twelve, finding myself ravenously and incessantly hungry, my friend, McCully Judd, would take me in his truck to the same Chinese cemetery in Manoa Valley where I would scavenge the grave stones and altars for something to eat. It did not seem so strange a pastime to either of us, but there were easier ways to obtain food. I was creating my own myth.

Near the end of Kamehameha III's reign in 1854, a movement was initiated by some of the missionary and mercantile families, despite ties of the monarchy to Great Britain, to ally the Islands more closely with the United States. Sixty years earlier, having been given a flag and a vague promise of protection by Captain Vancouver, Kamehameha I had informally ceded the Islands to Great Britain with the mistaken impression that this gesture of loyalty obliged the English to take his kingdom under its protection. This false confidence had not only given the Hawaiians a flag almost identical to the English flag, but had enabled Kamehameha I and John Young, his minister, to treat those foreigners who had designs on the Islands with a certain high-handed arrogance. This inclination toward England continued through the reign of Kamehameha's grandson, Alexander Liholiho, Kamehameha IV, whose wife, Emma, a granddaughter of John Young, was one of the founders of the Episcopal Church in Hawai'i. (When Kamehameha IV and Emma married, Queen Victoria sent a set of Copeland china and Napoleon III gave them an elaborate silver service.) As a young man, Liholiho and his older brother, Lot, had undertaken a Grand Tour of Europe, Asia, and America under the tutelage of Dr. G. P. Judd, ancestor of my friend McCully Judd. Unfortunately, the young men had been thrown out of a railway car in New York under the impression that they were Negroes, a gesture which did not further endear the United States to the princes.

Surprisingly, the Lymans and other powerful missionary families were opposed to the idea of annexation by the United States and Mrs. Lyman, whose own sons and friends were buying land as fast as they could when they were not stealing it, was made indignant by the grasping mainland Americans: "They [the Hawaiians] are the rightful owners of the soil and I do not like the idea of their being supplanted by wicked and designing men.... Great efforts have been made to bring about that event [annexation] and many of our foreign residents as well as Californians have confidently expected that it would take place. For the sake of the poor natives I am heartily glad they are disappointed."[5]

It was inevitable that the missionaries and their descendants take an interest in protecting the gradually emerging land system, especially as it promised great riches. "This is not said with a view to undervalue the services of the early missionaries to Hawaii," writes the Hon. R. M. Daggett, "but to show that all missionary fields have not been financially unfruitful to zealous and provident workers."[6] The historian John Dominis Holt is less sympathetic: "Some of the finest aspects of their Polynesian heritage predestined the Hawaiians to lose the race for economic supremacy. They were naively generous, predisposed from the first to be friendly to the whites who settled on their islands and lacked to a surprising degree the need to acquire status symbols."[7]

Bob Krauss, writing in the *Honolulu Advertiser*, takes a lighter view: "Actually the record shows that the missionary was a much better friend to the Hawaiian than the horde of haole seamen and traders who descended on the Islands

hoping to make a fast buck. One of the ways to make a for-
tune was in sugar. So the haole planted the land with sugar
cane. Then he found he didn't have enough hands to work the
fields. The Hawaiians preferred fishing to hard work and low
pay. The haole began importing labor.... That's how Hawaii
became populated."[8]

Rarely did the missionaries' children become missionaries themselves. After attending Punahou, the young men
were sent to New England to be further educated, usually at
Harvard or Yale; the girls went to finishing schools in San
Francisco or Chicago. The children of the missionaries and
planters returned to the Islands after college, married the
children of other missionaries and planters, and quickly and
easily began to make their own fortunes. One of the oppor-
tunistic haole men was another of Sarah Lyman's sons,
Frederick Lyman, who married Isabella Chamberlain, the
daughter of missionaries. "Mr. Lyman is another instance of
successful arrangement," writes the traveler Sophia Cracroft,
"not to say bargaining: he has some thousand or two of acres,
which he bought of the government at half a dollar an acre!
There is, however, some scandal attached to this transaction,
as Mr. Lyman was formerly a government surveyor and sur-
veyed this land.... Serious mistakes with regard to private
property were made by him ... and though in one instance
restitution on a large scale has had to be made, he retains
land which could not rightfully be sold.... Most of the missionaries are landholders on their own account and cultivate
their property. This necessarily occupies much of their time,
which should be given to the care of their people."[9]

LYMAN MUSEUM, HARRY A. WESSEL COLLECTION

Hilo, early 20th century: Children attended by Japanese servants

The grandson of Rev. Hiram Bingham, who was tutor to the boy king who banished the old gods in 1819, assumed a more worldly view. He married a rich relative of Louis Comfort Tiffany in New York City, and discovered Machu Picchu.

CHAPTER ELEVEN

The Kanaka Maoli

As King William Lunalilo did not name an heir before he died in 1874, Prince David Kalakaua, a descendant of ali'i advisors to Kamehameha the Great, was elected king by special session of the legislature. Two years later, a reciprocity treaty was enacted to guarantee that no trade tariffs with the United States would impede the rapid rise of the lucrative sugar industry. "Sugar is now the great interest of the islands," writes Isabella Bird. "Christian missions and whaling have had their day, and now people talk sugar. Hawaii thrills to the news of a cent up or a cent down in the American market.... The interests of the kingdom ... [are] clamorous in some quarters for 'annexation,' and in others for a 'reciprocity treaty,' which last means the cessions of the Pearl River lagoon on Oahu, with its adjacent shores to America, for a Pacific naval station.... In spite of a king and court, and titles and officials without number, and uniforms stiff with gold lace, and Royal dinner parties with menus printed on white silk, Americans, Republicans in feeling, really 'run' the government."[1]

King Kalakaua made valiant if meaningless attempts to restore the powers of the monarchy, including an insistence on such symbolic rights as the use of lighted torches by day, an honor allowed only to his family, but the haoles, having shrewdly secured the necessary power, barely troubled to dismiss the king as reactionary. "The two groups stood at opposite poles in the struggle for power," writes Holt. "Pride of independence, pride in keeping at least the illusion of rule in the land of their forefathers, kept Hawaiians fixed to their pole. A fierce desire to keep what had been acquired from long dedicated effort, a strong identification with their American roots, and an unfortunate conviction that native Hawaiians did not know what was good for them, gave the opposing side its raison d'etre."[2]

On King Kalakaua's return to the Islands from his bibulous trip around the world in 1881, he wrote a chant for his people entitled "Ka Momi." It is translated by Mary Kawena Pukui.

The Pearl

As I stood at the sides of heads of governments,
next to leaders proud of their rule, their authority
over their own,
I realized how small and weak is the power I hold.
For mine is a throne established upon a heap of lava.
They rule where millions obey their commands.

Only a few thousands can I count under my care.
Yet one thought came to me of which I may boast,
that of all beauties locked within the embrace of
   these shores,
one is a jewel more precious than any owned by my
   fellow monarchs.
I have nothing in my Kingdom to dread.

I mingle with my people without fear.
My safety is no concern, I require no bodyguards.
Mine is the boast that a pearl of great price has fallen
   to me from above.
Mine is the loyalty of my people.[3]

Isabella Field, the stepdaughter of Robert Louis Stevenson, fond friend and drinking companion of the melancholy Kalakaua, saw only the romance and beauty of the languid kingdom. "The plaintive, tender Hawaiian airs were lovely, and the hulas set to music ... made good lively tunes for the polka and schottische. But it was when they put down their instruments and sang! How well I remember the silken swish of long trains, the sound of feet slipping over the ballroom floor in time to the ... voices of the Royal Hawaiian Band!"[4] Historian Holt adds, "If ... nothing else, the king's staff handsomely embellished the social or storybook aspects of the last days of the Hawaiian monarchy. The extraordinary beauty of the part-Hawaiian wives and daughters, some of them dressed by Worth of Paris, added a further touch of the exotic."[5]

("The Royal Hawaiian Band ... proved difficult at first," writes Bob Krauss. "When bandmaster Berger arrived to organize the Royal Hawaiian Band in 1872, the only manpower available for the project were inmates of the reform school.... The 40 musicians assigned to Berger had never seen instruments before and could not read music. 'But,' he reported, 'they had musical ears.... Their eyes were quicker than their brains. Within a month they could play half a dozen melodies and a little waltz.'")[6]

Isabella Bird was also much beguiled by island life—her descriptions of Hilo could serve as a rendering of the Hawai'i that I know:

> I ... find this a very satisfactory life.... The white population here, which constitutes 'society' is very small.... Their houses combine the trimness of New England, with the luxuriance of the tropics; they are cool retreats, embowered among breadfruit, tamarind, and bamboo, through whose graceful leafage the blue waters of the bay are visible.... I never saw people live such easy, pleasant lives.... Light Manila matting is used instead of carpets.... One novel fashion is to decorate the walls with festoons of the beautiful *Microlepia tenuifolia,* which are renewed as soon as they fade, and every room is adorned with a profusion of bouquets.... Many of the residents possess valuable libraries ... with cabinets of minerals, volcanic specimens, shells and coral, with weapons, calabashes, ornaments and cloth.[7]

LYMAN MUSEUM, HARRY A. WESSEL COLLECTION

Hilo, early 20th century: Island society

Even Mark Twain, who complained in the letters he contributed to a Sacramento newspaper that King Kalakaua conducted "Pagan orgies,"[8] made his contribution to the myth, writing in 1894 a florid "Prose Poem on Hawaii": "No alien land in all the world has any deep, strong charm for me but that one: no other land could so longingly and beseechingly haunt me sleeping and waking, through half a lifetime, as that one has done. Other things leave me, but it abides; other things change, but it remains the same. For me its balmy airs are always blowing, its summer seas flashing in the sun; the pulsing of its surf-beat is in my ear; I can see its garlanded crags, its leaping cascades, its plumy palms drowsing by the shore; its remote summits floating like islands above the cloud-rack; I can feel the spirit of its woodland solitude; I can hear the plash of its brooks; in my nostrils still lives the breath of flowers that perished twenty years ago."[9]

The elegance and gaiety of the garden parties, the great charm of the women in their Paris gowns, and the increasing prosperity, comfort, and even glamour, was enjoyed only by the small world of the gentry—those descendants of the early missionaries and ship captains, and the few members of an Anglicized Hawaiian nobility and its courtiers. Holt describes Honolulu as barely stirring in its "usual state of smoldering melancholy."[10] The poet, Palea, born in 1852 on the Big Island, composed this chant, "Piano Ahiahi," upon hearing the foreigners' piano for the first time.

Piano at Evening

O Piano I heard at evening
where are you?

Your music haunts me far into the night
like the voice of landshells

trilling sweetly
near the break of day.

I remember when my dear and I
visited aboard the Nautilus
and saw our first looking glass.

I remember the upland of Ma'eli'eli
where the mists creeping in and out
threaded their way between the old
houses of thatch.

Again I chant my refrain
of long ago and a piano singing
far into the night.[11]

In the last decades of the nineteenth century, the population of native Hawaiians, Kanaka Maoli, had fallen to 40,000 people, the first time in the history of the Islands that its people were a minority. Isabella Bird, writing in 1873, was too sensitive not to see that "the dwindling of the race is a most pathetic subject.... The chiefs ... are a nearly extinct order; and with a few exceptions, those who remain are childless.... I came everywhere upon traces of a once numerous population, where the hill slopes are now only a wilderness of guava scrub, and upon churches and school-houses all too large, while in some hamlets the voices of young children were altogether wanting. This nation ... has to me the mournful aspect of a shrivelled and wizened old man dressed in clothing much too big, the garments of his once athletic and vigorous youth."[12]

The missionaries had proved all too effective. "There was death," writes John Dominis Holt, "and survival ... was determined by the degree they could accept ... the invading foreigner. Confused and weakened, the Hawaiian lost his resistance to death. Spiritually as well as physically, he was reduced to nothing."[13]

In 1959, when the birth statistics for all races in the Islands was 17,050 births, 4,673 of whom were Caucasian, only 114 births were of pure Hawaiian ancestry.[14]

CHAPTER TWELVE

The Queen

Despite the gradual but relentless usurpation and loss, Liliʻuokalani, chosen heir apparent by her brother, King Kalakaua, became queen in 1891 with the early death of Kalakaua in San Francisco where he had traveled for his health (the king's last words were whispered into an Edison recording machine: "Tell my people I tried").[1] Liliʻuokalani's short reign of two years was fraught with dissension and the threat of rebellion. When the queen, "brave though *paakiki* (stubborn),"[2] determined to end the restrictions placed on the crown by the far-sighted white businessmen, ranchers, and politicians by abrogating the Constitution of 1887 and demanding a new one, her haole ministers of state quickly formed a Committee of Safety to appoint a provisional government. Monarchy in the Islands had long been a charming *tableau vivant* permitted by those men happy to indulge the myth of the native nobility so long as business was not compromised. With Sanford B. Dole, a rich rancher, at its head (he who had shown his collection of skulls to Agassiz in Boston), the Committee of Safety simply declared in 1893 that the ancient line of Hawaiian kings was ended. Troops took the palace and the queen, in the interest of preventing bloodshed, was politely asked to surrender her crown.

The demise of the monarchy was accomplished with businesslike calm. Hawai'i was declared a protectorate of the United States and a committee was dispatched from Washington to negotiate a treaty of union. A group of royalists that had gathered as early as 1889 around King Kalakaua was hurriedly rallied by Robert Wilcox (a relative of the prosaic Miss Mabel Wilcox) on behalf of the queen. The haphazard resistance lasted ten days before Lili'uokalani was arrested for treason by the exasperated businessmen. Her only request was for clemency for the men who had supported her in a hopeless insurrection. In 1894, to general rejoicing (as had greeted the abolition of the gods in 1819), Hawai'i was declared a territory of the United States.

Sanford B. Dole, educated at Punahou and Williams College, became governor of the new territory. The first Territorial Legislature was elected in 1901 (about the time that hundreds were killed in a fire deliberately set in Chinatown to curb an outbreak of bubonic plague). In 1903, Theodore Roosevelt appointed George Carter the second territorial governor. Carter, a graduate of Yale who founded the Hawaiian Trust Company and the Hawaiian Fertilizer Company, was also a director of the powerful C. Brewer and Company. The third governor, Walter Frear, another graduate of Yale, was the director of numerous banking, sugar, pineapple, and railroad companies. Lawrence McCully Judd (another descendant of Dr. G. P. Judd), educated at Punahou, Hotchkiss, and the University of Pennsylvania, was seventh territorial governor in 1929. Judd was a director of Theo H. Davies and Company and manager of the Hawaiian Meat Company. William F. Quinn, the last territorial governor, in 1957, was a graduate of Harvard Law School. Other than the Hawaiian prince, Jonah Kuhio Kalanianaole, a descendant of the last king of Kaua'i and delegate to the United States Congress from 1902 to 1922, there was scant representation by nonwhites until Hiram Fong, a rich Chinese American, and Daniel Inouye, a Japanese-American war hero who had lost an arm fighting for the Allies, were elected to the United States Senate in 1959, the year that statehood was granted.

Upon release from detention, the queen retired to her house, Washington Place. "The sordid attempts to defame the queen's good name and to further degrade the character of the Hawaiian people are a sad consequence of revolution," writes Holt. "The ancestry of the queen, her morals, and her religious beliefs were garnered from sources originating in the gutters of island gossip and publicized in such a way as to cause one to wonder if the underlying currents which brought an end to Hawaiian monarchy were not more racial in character than they were political."[3]

In her memoir of Hawai'i, Helen Caldwell describes the deposed Lili'uokalani two years before the queen's death:

> She lives quietly at Washington Place in Honolulu, and though frail in health, at age 77 still takes much interest in the life of her people. In a visit to her

home recently I found her seated between two royal kahilis [feather staffs], with her lap full of roses, which enhanced the beauty of her white hair and the simplicity of her black holoku. She was most gracious and told with animation of her love for music, of the inspiration a composer feels, and of the meles that were written in honor of her ancestors according to the ancient customs. It was a great honor she conferred in sending for one of her old retainers, who with the admirable dignity of carriage and manner characteristic of the Hawaiian matron, appeared at the doorway in an immaculate white holoku and yellow feather lei, the royal insignia, and chanted in weird and long-sustained tones one of the royal meles only heard on state occasions. As she chanted and portrayed with many gestures, the scenes described, the queen explained the meaning thereof, and told how difficult of translation is the poetic thought embodied in the highly figurative language of the Hawaiians.[4]

Queen Lili'uokalani composed many meles and chants, among them the hula "Ka Wiliwiliwai," written on the lanai of Washington Place (the house in which, when I was fifteen, I had my first serious flirtation) when she saw for the first time the watering system of her neighbors, Dr. and Mrs. McKibbin. (Bob Krauss is rather hard on the queen: "A tremendous amount of Hawaiian music was simply stolen outright. 'Aloha Oe,' the best known of all Hawaiian songs, written by Queen

Liliʻuokalani … is an old hymn, 'Rock by the Sea,' with new words.")[5] "The Sprinkler" is full of *kaona,* or hidden meaning, and, while dancing it, the hips mimic the arc of the spray.

O whirly-water
gentle rain shower on the move
what do you think you're up to
circling, twirling so quietly?

You there! You there!
Yea, yea—coming up!
As you revolve,
when—oh, when
will you—will you—
will you ever hold still?

Amazing
the way you take over: irresistible.
Come, slow down a little—
so I can drink![6]

CHAPTER THIRTEEN

The Paradise

Hawai‘i was a ravishing little world in 1960 (or is that too a myth?).

It was an isolated place, redolent with romance. Two hundred thousand people lived in Honolulu; a rise, however, of almost 17 percent since 1950. (In 2025 the population of the city is expected to be one million people.) Before the development of jet air-travel in the late 1950s, it had been difficult to reach the Islands—five days by ship from San Francisco (Los Angeles did not exist for us; it was thought to be a little vulgar).

It was an hierarchical, snobbish, and quietly racist society. We attended the Punahou School—King Kalakaua tells several myths about the spring called Ka Punahou: "The Mountain Mist and Waahila Rain ... occasionally visited Punahou, which was under their especial care and protection; but when the land

and spring passed into the hands of foreigners, who did not pay homage ... and who allowed the springs to be defiled by the washing of unclean articles and by the bathing of unclean persons, the twins indignantly left the place, and retired to the head of Manoa Valley"[1]—as unclean persons. We left the Islands for university on the mainland and most of us returned; we married one another. This charming, even enchanting life of a mainly haole elite was to change, of course, but it lasted for a long time.

The houses in which I lived were not of spectacular design; most often a vernacular version of a colonial villa, or a farmhouse of a simplified New England Greek Revival style with slender columns and a tin roof, or an oversize California bungalow in the arts and crafts style, sometimes grand with a screened Greene and Greene sleeping porch and porte cochère like our gray shingled house in Tantalus. Some children, those who had parents who were architects or left-wing lawyers who represented longshoremen and other Communists, lived in more modern houses of poured cement and steel, one of which, I remember, was built rather snugly around a large monkeypod tree, suggesting that the growth of the tree had not been sufficiently calculated. Houses at the beach or in the mountains of Wai'anae, or Koke'e on the island of Kaua'i, were made of wood, well-constructed but extremely simple (not in a chic way), indistinguishable but for size from the cottages in the workers' camps built at the turn of the century by Japanese craftsmen, sometimes to sublime effect with carved eaves and porch posts and *tansu*-like cupboards of 'ohi'a wood. The houses in the mountains had large stone fireplaces; the beach houses

LYMAN MUSEUM

1950s: The Hawaii Visitors Bureau advertisement of the myth

and sometimes even the big houses had outdoor showers. Occasionally, a porcelain bathtub was placed in the jungly part of the garden and filled when necessary with rainwater that was stored in large wooden tanks. This water was a rusty reddish-brown color and we used it to wash our hair as well as to bathe. Mainland guests who were unaccustomed to the collecting of rain thought that we chose to wash in dirty water but, out of politeness, never complained, and we did not know to explain. I sometimes worried about the tourists. I did not understand why they had come so far, excluded as they were from the secret and mythical world that I knew, and I was made anxious by the ease with which they were satisfied—a boat ride around Pearl Harbor to look at the sunken warships and the Kodak Hula Show with dancers in cellophane skirts seemed to suffice. It was the first time that I was to be confused by the difference between what people were willing to accept and what more there was for the taking.

The maids were Japanese; the cook was Chinese, sometimes Filipino. The gardeners were Japanese and the yardmen often the descendants of Portuguese plantsmen from the Azores. Hawaiians were never servants or gardeners; they were sometimes, but rarely, lawyers or doctors or schoolteachers—not because they were discouraged or deterred, but because it held little interest for them. It did not occur to anyone that they wished to be what is called professional, and to all appearances, they didn't.

It took my young mother from Philadelphia, a newcomer then to the Islands, some time to relinquish her East Coast idea of how children ought to look and behave (sterling silver food pushers, like little hoes, to use before a knife was mastered, and

Makapuʻu, Oʻahu, 1953: The author's mother, Anne Moore, with a friend holding Anne's fourth child, Michael

tiny correspondence cards engraved with my initials suitable for enclosing with birthday presents). Big rectangular boxes noisy with tissue paper would arrive at the end of August from Best and Co. in New York with seersucker shorts and jackets for the boys, white linen blouses with red rickrack, plaid bathing costumes well elasticized, brown lace-up shoes, navy blue cardigans with faille trim, dresses smocked with little ducks, and piqué sun hats, but she gamely admitted her own particular failure of myth when we eventually rebelled and refused to wear the clothes. At home and when we were not at school, girls wore printed cotton muʻumuʻus in unusually bright patterns,

Tantalus, Honolulu, 1955: Mike Moore, dressed by Best and Co.

and Chinese pajamas with loose trousers, often of shantung or pongee, reaching to the middle of the shin. Twice a year, we were taken downtown to McInerny's where clothes would be laid out for our approval by solemn Japanese saleswomen. The McInernys had been early residents of the Islands and had done well, making it all the more thrilling to watch old Miss McInerny boldly steal girdles, bathing caps, and evening gowns and stuff them carelessly into worn, brown paper sacks. Each night, so we were told, Miss McInerny's maid collected all the things that the old lady had stolen that day and returned them to the store, a system that seemed to please everyone, including us. We wore leis whenever we could (during the Second World War, leimakers were put to work making camouflage nets), not only on special occasions, and flowers in our hair. Once freed of the Best and Co. boxes, my bathing suits were made for me at Linn's, a small shop on Lewers Avenue, a shaded side street off Kalakaua Avenue in Waikiki. The bathing suit was always the same: two-piece, made of white cotton duck or a yellowish sharkskin; the bottom not quite a bathing suit but not tennis shorts either, with two vertical rows of buttons that made a flap in front like that on a sailor's trousers, and two thin vertical grosgrain stripes down the outside of each leg, usually in navy or red. They were astonishingly smart.

I spent my entire childhood and adolescence at Punahou, as did all my friends and my brother. I did not know many children from other schools. There were a few private schools that were Catholic, which meant that mainly Puerto Rican, Portuguese, or Filipino children, segregated by gender (and segregated from us by social class and religion, even if we were

Catholic), were educated there. My second brother was a student at a private boys' school called Iolani. The Kamehameha School, quite a distance from Punahou, held great allure for us. The school had been established in the nineteenth century by the Bishop Estate (that of Princess Bernice Pauahi who founded the museum) for children of Hawaiian blood. The Kamehameha boys, often very beautiful, and inaccessible to us in a subtle and unspoken way, were splendid athletes. We imagined that they had a familiarity with a sexuality forbidden and even unknown to us, perhaps because of their beauty and grace, but more likely because they were handsome boys with brown skin. We held the Hawaiians in a confused (not articulated or even understood) reverence.

There was a great deal of travel between the islands. This was so, in part, because there were few schools other than Punahou and Kamehameha that took boarders. As a consequence, some of my friends came from ranches on the Big Island and plantations on Maui and Kaua'i (adults went to Moloka'i only to shoot the slender deer that flourish in the eastern mountains, introduced in 1869 by the Duke of Edinburgh who'd had them pressed on him by the Mikado of Japan) and I would go home with my friends during the long holidays and the summer. I learned to drive when I was thirteen in a surplus World War II Army jeep in the cane fields of Kaua'i—McCully Judd drove an Army tank, destroying beyond redemption Mrs. Johnson's garden when he lost control of the tank one afternoon. That kind of visiting does not happen much anymore, perhaps because there are more schools on Maui and Hawai'i now.

Hilo, 2001: Quack Moore, the wife of Rick Moore

New York, 1997: The author with her brothers, Rick and Mike

We were not asked to wear shoes to school until the sixth grade, with the result that I could walk like a fakir over anything, including broken glass. I wore cotton dresses and, when it was very hot, pinafores, the latter causing me much embarrassment until I refused to wear them—I was so convinced that my featureless chest was exposed that I held my arms pressed to my sides, making the use of a blackboard or a baseball bat difficult. We ate lunch in the school cafeteria which was in its own building; it was thought a bit scholarship-ish if you carried your lunch to school in a bag, or pail decorated with a cartoon figure. It was possible to sit under a big monkeypod tree in the courtyard; when the tree was in bloom, the petals dropped into your food. As at home, the menu was ecumenical—Spam, rice every day, *inari* sushi (which resembled the elbow skin of an old Japanese man), chicken *hekka,* tuna on damp white bread, *char siu* pork, Portuguese sausage, macaroni salad (known as mac), *malasadas* (sweet lumpy Portuguese doughnuts without holes), kimchee, Fritos, saimin (noodle soup) every day, beef teriyaki on bamboo sticks.

I was passionate about my teachers. Some of them were shockingly young (it was rumored that in the upper school, known as the Academy, there was clandestine dating between some of the girls and the teachers—as a student in the Academy myself one day, I can confirm that there was), in their early twenties, often from the East Coast, and I wonder if Honolulu was not a particularly good place to spend a year or two after leaving Yale and before moving on to a more suitable career (Viet Nam). In the second grade, I asked my teacher, Mrs. Corcoran, to have lunch with me one Saturday at the old Moana Hotel in Waikiki, signing my name to the check in a large left-handed scrawl. I have wondered why she agreed to go. I kept it a secret for many years. My fifth-grade teacher, a very attractive gentleman fresh from Williams, was, to my great distress, lost taking a dugout up the Sepik River in Papua New Guinea.

After school, we would leave the grounds through the lower gate covered with night-blooming cereus (which we did not see in bloom until we were much older, being asleep in our beds by the hour that the big, waxy flowers deigned to open) to buy penny candy, preserved seeds of mango, plum, and cherry called *see moi*, and white paper cones of shave ice flavored

Honolulu, 1962: At dinner with Robert Hemmeter, a history teacher at Punahou

with artificial syrups in fluorescent colors at a tiny grocery patronized by Punahou children for generations called the Chink Store because of our unquestioned devotion to the Chinese husband and wife who owned it. Away from school, I was sometimes chased by terrifying local girls called *titas* (from the Portuguese for "aunt") who, for sport, did not take to haoles—the excuse for a chase was usually the absurd accusation that I had been staring at them. The signal for me to run was when one of them shouted loudly, "What? I owe you money?"

Once a week, I attended cotillion at the Royal Hawaiian Hotel, held in a longhouse in the hotel's then enormous garden. I was once required to leave in disgrace for surreptitiously turning on the fire-prevention sprinkling system concealed in the thatch roof (I was caught because I was the only one not

Punahou School, Honolulu, 1955: The author is sitting on the railing.

drenched to the skin) and ruining everyone's painful patent leather pumps, and once I was asked to leave for secreting a hat pin in my white cotton glove, the better to prick the balloon decorations, thus causing our instructor, the red-haired Mrs. Wallace, to fall to the ground holding her bosom as if shot. The classes, although sweaty, were useful in the end. I and my dazed partner (it was a far worse experience for boys) bumped across the polished floor in stiff but enthusiastic renditions of the box step, later to be revealed as the fox-trot by the amused older men I began to dance with when I was fifteen, usually at weddings.

The food at home for children was not unlike the food given us at school. When our father and stepmother were in residence, I and my brothers and sisters ate at six o'clock every evening in the playroom (when our parents were away, we adopted a more convivial schedule with the connivance of the servants). We ate with adults only on occasions like Christmas or a birthday, and it was fairly excruciating. There was a great deal of rice. Our idea of dessert was sour *ume* (pickled cherries) or sweet egg sushi. We had no complaint, we loved rice, but it was not until I was much older that I had what I thought of as my first haole food. Food like artichokes and wiener schnitzel.

Ogo [seaweed] Salad

    1 cup fresh red ogo
    1 cup fresh green ogo
    1 cup brown ogo

For dressing:
1/4 cup shoyu
1/8 cup rice wine vinegar
1/2 cup sesame oil
1/4 teaspoon black pepper
1 large tomato, diced
1/2 finely chopped Maui onion
2 green onions, chopped, with tops
1 teaspoon grated fresh ginger

Bring a pot of water to a boil and blanch the ogo quickly. Remove and plunge into a bowl filled with ice water to cool. Squeeze out the excess water and pat dry. Put the ogo in a salad bowl with dressing. Chill before serving.

Kinau Wilder's Mango Chutney

Kinau Wilder, born into one of Hawai'i's most prestigious kama'aina [long-standing] families, was a beauty and an actress in her youth, an entrepreneur in early Waikiki nightspots in midlife, a delightful hostess always, and finally a mender of fine china par excellence.... This chutney is baked instead of cooked on top of the stove, and its origins can be traced to Hawai'i's early missionary families.

24 cups sliced fresh mangoes
5 pounds raw sugar
1 1-pound box seedless raisins

1 handful Hawaiian rock salt
1 head of garlic, peeled and minced
1 pint white vinegar
15 small red Hawaiian chili peppers
1 hand fresh ginger or 5 pieces the size of your thumb
1 teaspoon ground cinnamon
1 teaspoon nutmeg
1 teaspoon allspice
1 teaspoon ground cloves
1 tablespoon mustard seed
3 finely sliced lemons, seeds removed

Preheat the oven to 375°F. Peel and chop mangoes. Mix mangoes with raw sugar, raisins, and salt and place in a roasting pan. Chop up garlic, vinegar, chili peppers, and ginger. Add spices and lemon and mix. Combine with the mango mixture. Roast for three hours, stirring occasionally and checking to make sure it doesn't dry out. Add water as needed. Place in sterilized jars. Makes ten pints.

Kukuiolono Cocktail

There is a hill on the island of Kaua'i called Kukuiolono which means "the light of the god Lono." Sugar planter Walter McBride built his house atop this hill ... and like many a kama'aina ... became famous for his ... country hospitality.... This recipe has been adapted from the *Kaua'i Historical Society Cookbook*.

1 part gin
2 parts fresh peach or *liliko'i* [passionfruit] juice
sugar to taste
1 or 2 dashes of bitters
1 teaspoon orange juice

Mix the ingredients and shake well with ice. Makes 1 serving.

Auntie Robbie's Prune Crack Seed

Auntie Robbie St. Sure Apana always made her prune *mui* in large gallon mayonnaise jars.... She watched for packaged prunes and dried fruit such as apricots to go on sale at the local markets.

1 pound dark brown sugar
3 tablespoons Hawaiian rock salt
3 tablespoons bourbon
1 tablespoon Chinese Five Spice powder
2 cups lemon juice
8 12-ounce packages pitted prunes
2 12-ounce packages dried apricots or mixed dried fruit
1/2 pound Chinese dried lemon peel, cut into small pieces
1/2 pound seedless *li hing mui*

In a large bowl, combine sugar, salt, bourbon, Five Spice, and lemon juice. Toss in prunes and other dried fruit, lemon peel, and li hing mui. Place in a clean gallon jar to soak. Let stand for a minimum of four days, mixing twice a day.[2]

On the weekends, we went into the mountains, depending on the season, to pick ginger and to dig up rare ferns to grow in pots, and to float down the flumes, absolutely forbidden to us, that carried the cold mountain water that irrigated the pineapple and cane fields. The wooden flumes, often on trestles and sometimes running underground, were lined with leeches that I picked from my bare legs and shirtsleeves when I emerged breathless from the chute. There was a myth that you would be chopped to pieces by the metal blades of a waterwheel should you not remove yourself from the flume in time—oddly enough this was said to have happened only to Japanese girls, suggesting that they were not so agile; not so thoroughly island girls as ourselves. I twice broke my wrist (the same wrist) fluming. The second time I was afraid to tell my father, who was a doctor, because he had warned me to be careful until my first fracture had healed. I made a cast for myself in the garage out of wet newspapers and paste and went in to supper and vomited on the table. If it had been raining, we went *ti*-leaf sliding down the muddy and precipitous ditches made by the ancient Hawaiians for sledding called *he'e holua* (the dangerous slides are now abandoned; the Visitors Bureau put in telephone poles midway down each slide to discourage tourists after one of them was killed—what was he doing there in the first place? we asked indignantly) or to the beach, either to the Outrigger Canoe Club which was private and then in the center of Waikiki, next to the Royal Hawaiian Hotel, or to Sandy Beach, or Makapu'u Beach at the eastern point of O'ahu where one of the goddess Pele's petroglyphs sits high on the cliff, overlooking the bay.

Honolulu, 1977: The author and her daughter, Lulu Sylbert

The beaches away from Waikiki were empty but for the occasional badly sunburned enlisted boys from the mainland in inappropriate bathing shorts who had wandered innocently into the dangerous surf on a quick round-the-island jaunt. By 1970, however, the pale Japanese girls who could no longer be kept at home by old-fashioned parents began to appear at Makapuʻu. They were still very Japanese with their neat pony-tails and baskets of sunscreen and lip salve. They kept apart, but the very fact that they were watching their boyfriends in the surf made me wonder where they had been all those years when my friends and I had been the only ones on the beach. Perhaps they'd been in sewing class or Japanese language school. I could not imagine what their grandmothers thought of them. It was an early lesson in the conflict of democratization.

The Outrigger Canoe Club, Waikiki, 1958: The author's parents, Anne and Richard Moore

If there were ten Japanese girls lying on the beach, there were ten fewer Japanese girls who still wore kimono and geta, who knew how to play the samisen, and arrange cherry blossoms in a way no haole could ever devise—but was that too a myth? The playing of the samisen was unknown to these girls' grandmothers, who had been brought to Hawai'i to labor in the fields. They could not resort to any instrument after twelve hours in the pineapple fields, their fingers horribly slashed. I wondered if it were a wonderful, if inevitable thing to wear a pink gingham bikini rather than a hobbled silk robe. Although Mrs. Gerould wrote that "it is impossible to be afraid of any one who wears a kimono, and that fact may be either our salvation or our undoing in our relations with the Orient,"[3] it could no longer be said that the most sensual part of a Japanese woman was the nape of her neck.

When I was nine, I was taught to ride a surfboard in Waikiki by the beach-boy Rabbit Kekai (who still surfs; his picture was in the *New York Times* recently in an article about elderly surfers) on a long wooden board. Ankle bands that attached by plastic cord to the board had not been invented. Neither Rabbit nor myself found it unseemly or even uncomfortable to assume our position—I would lie on my stomach facing the front of the board with my legs pleasantly spread so that he could slide on behind me. He also lay on his stomach, between my legs, his chin resting on my bottom. We both used our arms to paddle out to the break at Queen's Surf.

Although I would like to claim fluency in that most humorous and inventive of languages, pidgin English—like black street talk, it is always witty, always invigorated with imaginative new words—I and my haole friends only interspersed our conversation with words of pidgin English, as well as words of Hawaiian. We could speak pidgin, which I am pleased to say is considered by linguists to be a discrete language with a grammar and structure of its own, if required, and we could improvise, but it was not our native language. There were, however, certain words that Island people did not use. "Cold cuts" was not an Island expression. "Debutante" and "pasta" were mainland words. It was not that these words did not apply—nonapplicable words was another category altogether, with entries like "basement" and "galoshes." Some Hawaiian words that were a part of our vocabulary:

auwe! ouch or alas

haole white

hapa haole part-white

huhu trouble

kama'aina a longtime resident of the Islands

kapakahi uneven or crooked

kaukau food

lanai bower or porch

mahu male homosexual

makai toward the sea

make dead, pronounced MUCK-ay

mauka toward the mountains, pronounced MAO-ka in two
   syllables, an exception to the rule that each vowel is enunciated

okole buttocks

opu stomach

pau finish or complete

palaka a coarse cotton plaid much beloved, in blue or red
   most commonly, first worn by cowboys and field workers.
   (a Kaua'i shirt, once my daily costume, was a soft blue
   chambray workshirt with long sleeves

pilau dirty or stinky

pilikia trouble

puka hole

(Until recently, I had never heard anyone other than a
flight attendant or someone who worked behind the desk at a
Waikiki hotel say the now ubiquitous *mahalo*—thank you.)

Some of the pidgin English words that we used, taken from

Japanese, Korean, Filipino, Portuguese, and Samoan, among other languages:

babooze a fool
bambucha breasts
boy-flower anthurium
buckaloose breaking free
bumbye later
but however or though, used at the end of a sentence as in
   "he gone grind but," meaning "he is eating, however"
cha-langa-lang Hawaiian music
cockaroach steal
daikon leg legs that are short, white, and fat
fattabull very large person
fut fart, although, worryingly, fut-less means confused
get have, as in "I get one headache"
giri-giri cowlick
jam up messed up
Mr. Chang tight trousers, after the legendary bandleader
   at Punahou
manong Filipino
moke local boy
no mention you're welcome
puff blow, as in "puff your nose"
shaka hello, accompanied by a clenched fist, the forefinger
   and baby finger extended
shi-shi urine
side place, as in "she stay Waikiki side"
spark see

stink-ear a disposition to hear the bad, although stink-eye
means a dirty look
tita local girl, aunt
wahine sick venereal disease (an old plantation word)
zori rubber slipper (A zori with velvet straps is called a
prom flip; one with very thick soles is a kamaboko flip
after the Japanese word for "fish cake.")

We rarely took lessons outside of school, and there was little organized sport. All questions as to precedence or selection were decided by playing *Junk an' a Po,* a game of scissors, stone, and rock; three out of five rounds were sufficient to settle almost anything. My Japanese friends went to Japan School in the late afternoon so as not to forget their heritage, although I never heard any of them speak Japanese, nor did they seem overly interested in their heritage. If a Japanese girl were caught with a boy who was not Japanese, however, she would disappear overnight—only years later did we realize that she'd been whisked to Japan for safekeeping. (Kidnapping was also employed to dispose of unmarried girls who became pregnant, some of whom only returned to the Islands as grown women, having long given up their illegitimate child for adoption.) An elderly, rather elegant French woman, always dressed in damp pastel chiffon and a large flowered hat, was my French tutor. She gave genteel but nonetheless intriguing hints that her position in life previous to that of tutor to restless children in the tropics had been somewhat more distinguished, if not downright glamorous. It was not until years later, sitting in a dark movie theater, that I recognized Madame as lady's maid to Luise Rainer in *The Great Ziegfeld.* One very hot summer, I was inexplicably compelled by my mother to take sewing lessons from a Japanese seamstress in downtown Honolulu, an ambitious although slightly loony project. No thought was given as to just how I was to reach Mrs. Kimura's rooms with the result that a two-hour bus ride, each way, was necessary. I sewed a brown-and-white plaid sleeveless dress made of shagbark (does such a material still exist?) with a brown cummerbund that I wore to shreds even though the hem had been finished with masking tape. I considered any outing with my father to be sublime. I wrote in a novel in 1982, "Once a week, at night, Lily's father took her to the local high school to see National Geographic travelogues.... Lily sat next to her father in the front seat of his car. She even wore shoes for the special occasion and she trembled with pleasure. She kept her hands folded, ladylike, in her lap. The program always began, when the lights went out, with the words, 'We take you back in time, to a place as yet untouched by the modern world.' One particular program that electrified Lily was a tour of Olde Denmark. The song about wonderful, wonderful Copenhagen ran through her head for days. The evenings at the travelogues filled her with restlessness."

I was not given much spending money (I remember saving to buy a small brown paper sack of raisins) and indeed I did not need it. My mother was not only generous when necessary, but could effortlessly enter the imagination of a child, despite the Best and Co. brown shoes. When I was ten, I determined the need for a professional portrait and took myself to the studio of a Japanese photographer that I'd often passed on my bus ride home. He did not speak English—his business was mail-order bride portraits, I soon realized—but he did not question my somewhat odd request, which I demonstrated with hand signs and a few words of pidgin English. Nor did my mother question it when I asked her for the exorbitant sum of money he demanded for rather too many girlish poses (eighteen), nine of them with my chin resting lightly in my palm.

I did not have many possessions. For some time, I was bewitched by a wooden dollhouse; a chalet from Switzerland, complete with tiny red velvet geraniums in pots and a clean cow barn with minuscule bundles of straw and threadlike brown leather halters hanging on painted hooks. A cloth doll from Jamaica with gold earrings and a bright red cotton head wrap, the kind of curio sold on cruise ships, held my attention for quite some time. I played with the doll and the house, wildly mismatched and the doll three times the size of the house, for perhaps too long, but I had little other than an endless supply of books, which was literally my salvation, and a large, slightly shabby, due to its constant employment, Madame Alexander doll made in the image of Elizabeth II (rhinestone tiara, sky-blue Sash of the Garter, long white gloves) given me on the occasion of the queen's coronation in 1953.

We were rarely taken to a restaurant, and then only on a Sunday night for Chinese food. There was little television—*Captain Honolulu,* a cartoon show, was much admired—and only on the weekend. Sunday evening at six o'clock, servants and children watched television together, both contingents intensely loyal to a local program called *Televi Digest* in which people (not haoles) did laborious magic tricks or sang and

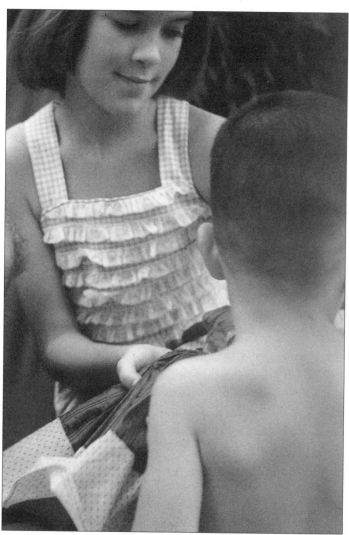

Honolulu, 1954: The author allows her brother Rick a look at the Jamaican doll.

danced for prizes. Our transistor radios were much valued. Listening to the adults' long-playing records, we knew every word of the songs in *Carousel, Ahmal and the Night Visitors,* and *Pal Joey.* We did not have much use of the telephone. Later, when we might have availed ourselves of it, the placement of the children's telephone in the kitchen did not encourage private conversation, which may have been the intention.

Bicycles were important. We often rode our rusty (the sea air) Schwinns to the old Waialae Country Club for lunch. As the club did not really get busy until the mysteriously named Happy Hour, we were able to commandeer one of the rickety green-felt card tables in the deserted Game Room, consuming egg salad sandwiches and Country Club Ice Tea (the *d* is not used at the end of a word in pidgin; it is "use cars" and "barbecue chicken") made with pineapple juice and mint, until we had played a few vicious rounds of greasy cards, at which point I signed the check and we decamped. It would be wildly self-dramatizing to say that we ate off the land, but, depending on the season, we did help ourselves freely (like Captain Cook's Indians) to whatever was growing—mangoes, lichees, tart lady apples, Surinam cherries, liliko'i, guavas, oranges, bananas, wild strawberries in patches congested with poison-spewing toads, wild mint, and wild watercress. There were one or two flowers that were unusually delicious to eat.

There were no fences, no locked gates, no marked boundaries or property lines, and we rode our bikes or roamed unconcerned through woods and plantations—to swim at Jackass Ginger pond in Nu'uanu, it was necessary to pass through many private gardens before reaching the waterfall. Much time, often at night, was spent in the trees, or on the beach, despite the mosquitoes and sand fleas, accompanied by two of our dogs, ungroomed and slightly foul-smelling (the salt water) black poodles, who were not then required to be on leads. We climbed the mountain called Koko Head, once named Kohelepelepe or Vagina Labia Minor—the fire goddess Pele was saved from being raped there by the pig-warrior Kamapua'a when her occasionally loyal sister, Hi'iaka, displayed her vagina to distract him—once innocently breaching the perimeter that a brigade of Marines had established in a war game and, to the curses of the officers, occasioning the failure of the operation.

I kept a large pet spider partly out of affection and partly to eat insects. She sat on my shoulder, retiring under my clothes to sleep. A red thread was tied to one leg (hers) so that I could haul her to safety should I wish to swim or lie down. I finally sat on her, and was somewhat relieved to be rid of her.

My youngest sister was placed eight months after her birth in my wicker bike-basket (lined in blue-and-white palaka) and accompanied us on all our jaunts. It is not an exaggeration to say that until she was two years old she lived by day in the bike-basket. I soon determined that it was too much trouble to pack and to change her cumbersome nappies (especially as there had been talk about the missing gross of diapers that I had tossed into the bushes when soiled), so she was naked. When we'd finished our gallivanting for the day, both she and the wicker basket were briskly hosed down.

It was in the ocean, though, that I felt as if I were, each time and at last, the self my heart would have chosen had it been asked. I swam in the morning and again in the early

Honolulu airport, 1959: The author, with a cast on her wrist, Mike, Rick, and Anne, she who resided in the bike-basket, meet their aunt, Miss Mary M. Shields.

afternoon. I swam at sunset. I would swim until I was tired, although not too tired to make it back to the beach. I found a hole in the reef into the deep water at the edge of the channel. If I swam far enough, I could see the big rock on the side of the mountain that marked the site of the shark-god's burial place. Sometimes I was overcome by an inexplicable feeling of panic, as if there were too much beneath and above me. I feared that the ocean might suddenly curl me into a wave and fling me from the loneliness of Earth into the loneliness of space, and I would hurry back through the reef as if the ocean were trying to catch me. One summer, when my mother was not well, we stayed on the beach in Punalu'u on the north shore of O'ahu. I grew convinced that I could see parts of bodies on the clean floor of the ocean and for some time, and to everyone's bafflement, I would not go into the water.

I am quite sure that adults had a very good time. There was lots of drinking; certainly infidelity, although the latter was unseen by most children. The one girl in our class at Punahou whose mother was divorced was tormented unmercifully and soon turned to horses rather than schoolmates for companionship. There was little interracial marriage among the white gentry, even if the great beauty of Polynesian women is attributed to the many strains of East and West running through their blood. Women wore more elaborate mu'umu'us than did girls, often made by a designer at the Royal Hawaiian Hotel called Pauline Lake, whose name I found very romantic, and narrow-brimmed straw hats modeled after the hats worn in the nineteenth century by Hawaiian ladies, with shell or feather bands, made by a fashionable milliner in Waikiki named Elsie

Das. (I may have her name wrong, but I will be corrected, I know.) Men wore rather boxy silk or rayon aloha shirts, not tucked into the trousers, as did boys, although the boys' aloha shirts were made of cotton. Boys, but not men, wore T-shirts.

There were no visible Jews or visible homosexuals of either sex; one or two blacks in the military. The military families were considered a bit lower-class. The girls were quite startling. They were flirtatious, accustomed to being around thousands of men conveniently organized into ranks. They were almost always blond and they wore Dr. Scholl's sandals to school. Raised in a hierarchy that was blatant, they were, unlike us, unembarrassed by ambition. They were also thought to be a little fast, but that wasn't why they were never quite accepted. It was island snobbery. The disdain of the clerisy.

There was a fairly unconscious racism all around us, although not toward Hawaiians, perhaps because they were not competitive. We thought them above approach, at any rate. We were unaware that the racism had long been institutionalized, but our parents and teachers knew, and sanctioned the restrictions and bylaws that kept non-haoles not only from private clubs, but from certain neighborhoods. These restrictions are ended now (sometimes by court decision), but in 1958 they were unquestioned by either side. I was astonished to learn that only haoles were allowed to live in the most desirable neighborhoods—Diamond Head and Kahala, for example—especially as there were three generations of Hawaiian fishermen, quite a number of children and dogs, and an irritable but dignified *tutu* (grandmother) in black holoku, *ilima* lei, and trim straw hat who lived in a compound on the beach at the bottom of our garden in

Kahala. "Squatters," my uncle explained when asked about this mysterious and jolly family. I spent quite a bit of time with them. Years later, I went to see the Worthingtons (descendants of an English sea captain? You see the dangers of myth), but they had disappeared. My uncle does not remember them. In 1970 a friend of mine (she who saved the turtle) had a love affair with a young Hawaiian man whom she met only at Makapuʻu Beach to bodysurf and to sneak into the lifesaving equipment hut to make love under an overturned dinghy—an arrangement that suited them both.

Despite (or because of) the unacknowledged divisions of class and race, there was no ostentation of wealth or power. Women did not wear jewels (or even dresses); no one drove an expensive car, nor indulged in visibly fancy vice. A few people were worldly enough to collect very good Asian art, which could be had for a song, especially after the war, and the fall of the Kuomintang government in China. If a holiday trip were made, it was not to Paris, but to Melbourne or Denver. Older women were addressed by their first name, preceded by Miss or, less formally, Auntie. A friend of mine, now in her eighties, is known as Auntie Sis. Her own sisters were Auntie Red and Auntie Old Lady (her name even as a girl). They are the descendants of a young sailor shipwrecked in the Islands in the nineteenth century and found asleep on the beach, naked, by one of the king's daughters who at once desired to marry him—a myth reminiscent of Odysseus and Nausicaa. Auntie Sis, as do those women of her age and class who are still alive, speaks with an antiquated aristocratic accent, somewhat English, passed down from the Yankee missionaries and Scots cabin boys who were her ancestors. "Do you remembah when we use to swim the hosses?" she will ask. "You were a little gel then."

Although the Hawaiians were admired and even idealized, there was little interest in Hawaiian culture. We learned hula, but it was always a hapa-haole hula, like "My Little Grass Shack" or "Lovely Hula Hands." A Hawaiian woman, Miss Alice, who sometimes looked after us when our father and stepmother were away, at my insistence taught me over the years the Hawaiian words of the old songs (oddly, I did not then know their meaning, either in Hawaiian or English, having learned by rote). She told me angrily (I could not tell: Was she angry with the Hawaiians or with me?) that the people had turned away from everything; the beautiful as well as the practical. Her great-grandfather had been interpreter of omens for a chief of O'ahu, but her children could not speak Hawaiian. She was perversely pleased that many of the old secrets had been lost—the location of the 'ape'ape herb found only in the damp mountain gullies of east Maui or the recipe for the love potion made from the last remaining stalks of red sugarcane. She said that there were very few people left who could speak with any certainty about the past. "The old meles and the old hero-tales are nearly forgotten, as are the old hulas," wrote Mrs. Gerould fifty years earlier.

> A few aged men and women can still sing and dance in traditional fashion ... but there is no one to whom they can pass on the words of the songs or the motions of the dance. The new songs are different—lyrical at best, never epic; and the new

dances might perhaps delight a cabaret, if any cabaret could conceivably by allowed to present them.... The old hulas were different; were stately and, I dare say, a little tiresome, with their monotonous swaying and arm gestures repeated a thousand times. Only a very old person now can dance in the earlier fashion; you could easily count up the Hawaiians who know the meles; and there is just one man, I believe, left on Oahu (if indeed he is still living) who can play the nose-flute as it should be played, to the excruciation of every nerve in a Caucasian body.[4]

By the end of the 1960s, we seldom went to Waikiki—once suburban shopping malls were built and the Outrigger Canoe Club moved to its present place near Diamond Head, there was no reason to go there. Only tourists and hustlers went to Waikiki. Alternative roads were built so that we did not even have to drive through Waikiki. We seldom went downtown except for trips to the dentist or doctor with an office in the old Alexander Young Hotel Building (the coffee shop famous for coconut-cream pies, packed in pale pink boxes to take home).

Not everyone felt the same curiosity about Hawai'i and its culture and history that possessed me; my parents and their friends preferred swimming in a chlorinated pool to the ocean and traveled to San Francisco sooner than to Hilo. The study of Hawaiian culture, and the awareness of a specific and important history was to come in the 1980s, to the point that many activists today demand the sovereignty of a

Hawaiian nation. Many of my friends now learn to speak Hawaiian, to dance hula with a strict *kumu hula* (teacher), to make Hawaiian quilts (in old times, said Miss Alice, the pattern came to a woman in a dream), to cook luau, to build outrigger canoes by hand. It is fashionable for haole men to belong to local clubs that race ocean canoes. In the 1950s, however, Hawaiiana was not yet a business. Stores did not possess large sections given to calendars of Filipino beach-boys, and cookbooks with imaginative breadfruit recipes, and anthologies of local murders—the result of an increase in tourism as well as the growing sense of a Hawaiian identity. The happy result, however, even if it is tinged with postmodernist interpretation or New Age philosophy (the practice of the latter largely confined to Maui, which is why I no longer go there), is the new scholarship and the publication of many good books. Muʻumuʻus are no longer worn, however. Some of the women who have lunch at the Outrigger Canoe Club wear Chanel suits, high heels, jewelry, and stockings—I must admit that in my own provincial way I am very shocked by the stockings. In India, I have noticed, many women have forsaken the sari for the *salwar kameez,* but that is about ease of movement and comfort, the opposite of the muʻumuʻu, which, in the end, turned out to be extremely practical as well as comfortable. The irony—of course—is that the disappearance of everything is just what has allowed us to see it.

CHAPTER FOURTEEN

The Musician

Punalu'u is the district known to be the haunt of the god Kamapua'a who, before Freud but after Herodotus, could take the shape of a pig or a handsome man—while a pig, he destroyed the lands of the ali'i; while a man, he seduced their women. "Leaving his horse at the termination of the valley and entering this narrow pass of not over fifty or sixty feet in width, the traveller winds his way along, crossing and recrossing the stream several times, till he seems to be entering into the very mountain.... One is stopped by a wall of solid rock rising perpendicularly ... to the height of some two hundred feet, and down which the whole stream must have descended in a beautiful fall.... The smooth channels ... are said to have been made by [Kamapua'a].... Old natives still believe that they are the prints of his back.... A party who recently visited the spot states that when they reached the falls they were instructed to make an offering.... This was done in true Hawaiian style; they built a tiny pile of stones on one or two large leaves, and so made themselves safe from falling stones, which otherwise would assuredly have struck them."[1]

One summer, my brother Rick, who was then twelve years old, stayed at Punalu'u with Dr. Welles and his family in a large house on the beach. Dr. Welles, who was part Hawaiian, and his haole wife, had managed to hold fast to a part of old Hawai'i. In the first light (sometimes in the dark with torches), we searched for any blue-glass balls that might have broken free from fishing nets in the Sea of Japan to float heedlessly across the Pacific to wash ashore at high tide. During the day, we collected *limu* (seaweed) and went spearfishing and prized *opihi* (tiny snails) from the ledges of the rock pools. It was not only in occupation and food that the Welles were old-fashioned, but in their *ho'okipa,* or generosity. We ate at a long wooden table on the lawn. It was impossible to know how many places to set until the last moment—often there were twenty people for dinner. Late at night, the *pune'es* and *hickie'es,* sleeping platforms that had been used as backless sofas during the day, were transformed into beds with the addition of pillows and light straw mats or quilts (no sheets) for any guests who chose to stay the night or could not make it home.

Early one evening, the Hawaiians who lived nearby strolled across the lawn with their bottles of *okolehao* (homemade swipe most often made from fermented pineapple) and ukuleles and guitars. Most of the Hawaiian men that we knew

Honolulu, 1964: The author at seventeen

worked for the city and county repairing the roads, or as entertainers at the clubs and hotels in town, or as small subsistence farmers and fishermen. (One of my Hawaiian friends insisted that Hawaiians were not working class. The working class wanted satellite dishes and motorboats, but Hawaiians didn't want anything.) The sun had not yet gone down, and the men and children carried chairs and wooden benches onto the lawn. Among the men was the musician Gabby Pahinu'i, who worked on the road crew. There was beer, and reeking cuttlefish, and sashimi. After a few hours of talking-story, Pahinu'i began to play slack-key guitar. He sang in Hawaiian and the other men played with him; some of the women, one at a time, rose to dance hula on the grass. The singing and dancing lasted through the night. "We have several times … been kept awake by the natives … talking and singing till near daybreak. Circumstances the most trivial sometimes furnish conversation for hours. Their songs also afford much amusement…. It is probable that many of the fabulous tales and songs so popular among them, have originated in the gratification they find in thus spending their time," wrote William Ellis in 1823.[2]

I awoke on the grass the next morning, rolled in a mat damp with dew. The men had gone to work. Dr. Welles was at

Hanalei, Kaua'i, 1994: The author and her brother Rick at a wedding on the lawn

the clinic. I washed in the outdoor shower, and my brother and I went fishing. I was aware that while I didn't yet understand what it meant to be attached to this Earth, I did not want to make the mistake of imagining that myth was something available to everyone. I understood that myth was a luxury.

CHAPTER FIFTEEN

The Grove

Last Christmas, on Moloka'i, I spent a month on a ranch on the top of a hill at the far eastern end of the island overlooking the bay of Halawa. The road goes no farther than Pu'u O Hoku, the "hill of stars." It is cool at night, and there is the sound of the wind moving through the ironwood, bringing the scent of eucalyptus. There are cattle on the mountainside, and horses and small animals—rats and mongoose, toads and bats. Halawa, once a large fishing and farming village, flourished in the tenth century. A river fed by numerous waterfalls winds through a narrow valley overgrown with guava, banana, coffee bushes, and ginger. A short distance into the forest, there are traces of taro patches and house foundations, and the stone ruins of altars and shrines. "[Papa heiau] ... is a rambling structure," according to the Moloka'i Site Survey. "A collection of

The Grove, Moloka'i, 2001: The author and John Newman

small platforms, terraces and walls, suggesting more the site of a college of priests than a heiau.... Located on the northern side of Halawa Valley, [Mana heiau] is by far the most imposing heiau structure in the valley.... {Built by the Menehune}, it was for human sacrifice."[1]

Moloka'i is small (only thirty-seven miles from west to east; ten miles in width), and the population remains much what it has been for two hundred years, perhaps five thousand people. The land is forested or used for agriculture. The first Protestant mission was founded in 1832. The use of an inaccessible peninsula on the north shore for the leper colony, Kalaupapa, has added to the island's mystery and its isolation, despite its nickname, The Friendly Isle, surely a fantasy of the Visitors Bureau. Kaunakakai, the capital, is a dusty cowboy town of a few hundred people with three streets of wooden buildings with false pediments. A hotel, now closed, did not open on the dry west end until 1977.

For some years, I have sought the sacred grove, Ulukuku'i o Lanikaula, on my walks along the cliff overlooking the sea, but I have never been fully satisfied that I've found the exact place of the seer Lanikaula's encampment, said to be a luminous grove of the silver-leafed *kuku'i* or candlenut tree. Lanikaula was a sorcerer of Maui who sought refuge on Moloka'i in the sixteenth century. He is said to be buried in the kuku'i grove. "Here he lived in seclusion and acquired a great reputation as a prophet and counsellor, so that from all the group [of islands], pilgrims came to the grove to seek advice and register vows; the latter process consisted in cutting a gash in one of the kukui trees forming the grove, and in the slit placing a lock of the votary's hair which was soon cemented there by the gum exuded by the tree."[2] The kuku'i tree is sacred to the Hawaiians and the source of endless gifts to them. The hollowed nuts were filled with their own oil and strung in a line on stiff fronds, burning for a minute or two before extinguishing themselves one by one. The leaves and bark were used for medicine; the inner bark made a permanent bloodred dye and a gum secreted by the tree was used to varnish kapa cloth. The black or mottled-brown nuts are still highly polished and strung on black ribbon for sale in tourist shops.

I have also spent years looking for the Vagina Rock that is companion to the splendid Phallic Rock in the mountains, but the Vagina Rock has been so long abandoned in a thicket of cedar, so overgrown with roots that I fear it is lost forever. "If you pass through Kualapu'u to the forest," says Harriet Ne, "you can see the great rock six feet high which is called Kaule o Nanahoa, which means 'the penis of Nanahoa.' Nanahoa was a prince who ... protected the rock because it was on his property. Also, it was precious to his people because it was known to cure infertility. But for him—and not only for him—it was a sorrow. He was married to a beautiful woman, and they were very happy until another woman came from another district. Nanahoa did not resist her loving glances, and soon they became lovers. The heart of his wife burned hotly within her; and when she found them together at the rock, she cried out in rage and hurled bitter accusations at them. Then she sprang at the woman and pushed her down the cliff. Even today, if you go there, you will find a perfectly formed female rock. I myself have seen it."[3] I have not.

One late afternoon last Christmas, my friends and I set out, once again, to find the place of Lanikaula's sacred grove on our three-mile walk to the bird sanctuary. The family to whom Pu'u O Hoku belongs has established a sanctuary on a grassy bluff overlooking the Cape of Halawa for the endangered nene goose (the same species that Douglas shipped to Kew Gardens), one of the few animals known to be endemic to the Islands. On the verge of extinction in the 1940s, much attention, some of it sentimental, has been given to saving the idiosyncratic little goose. One of its virtues is its ability to make its home on lava, without a source of water. It does not have much webbing between its toes.

I had begged more detailed directions from the Hawaiian woman who looked after us. Surprised that I was having so much trouble finding the grove, she explained once again: "Go

Moloka'i, 2001: Kiki atop the Phallic Rock of Nanahoa

up the cattle road, through the eucalyptus, take the down fork when you reach the bend and there it is." I had done that many times, and still I had not come upon the sacred grove. This time, however, she let slip an additional detail: "There is an old fence around it."

In Greek myth, Pasiphaë, She Who Shines for All, the wife of the Cretan king, Minos, beseeched of the exiled Daedalus, a sculptor of inventions and maker of toys for the royal children (among them Ariadne), a sculpture of a cow into which Pasiphaë could fit herself. She had fallen in love with a beautiful white bull and could not rid herself of a consuming passion for it. Daedalus obliged her in secret, making a lovely cow in which Pasiphaë could conceal herself. The cow with Pasiphaë inside was placed in a field and soon gained the notice of the beautiful white bull. He mounted the cow again and again, thus giving the queen the pleasure and release that her feverish desire required. In time, a child she conceived with the bull was born, the Minotaur, who possessed the body of a man and the head of a bull. Shamed by this proof of his wife's betrayal, Minos had Daedalus contrive a labyrinth in which the Minotaur could be imprisoned. (Although the myth of Pasiphaë and the bull is a metaphor for the ritual marriage held under an oak tree to affirm the union of the moon-priestess, wearing a diadem of cow's horns, and the Minos-king, wearing a mask to resemble a bull, and the labyrinth is thought to be Minos's enormous palace in Cnossus with its many doors and winding passages, I choose to believe in the Minotaur.)

It came as a surprise that I had walked past the grove many times—I'd rested beside it, and once fallen asleep in the weedy field that surrounds it. The kukuʻi is not a rare tree and it is easily seen from a distance thanks to its silver leaves. I had imagined that the sacred grove would announce itself in a blaze of light and a rustling of spirits, but the grove was commonplace. The barbed-wire fence was partly obscured by brush, but even had the grove been in the open, it did not appear distinguished. Certainly not sacred. What a lovely trick!

That afternoon, my friend Kiki was wearing, as she tends to do, a pleated black Issey Miyake dress that reached to her ankles, thin sandals and the heavy, jingling silver anklets of an Indian *apsara*. I was wearing khaki breeches in anticipation of riding with the cowboys. My friend, John Newman, a sculptor, and my daughter, Lulu, in a white nightgown, having just awakened, walked with us.

The fence around the field was so old that the rust rubbed off on my palms when I held down the knotted wire so that the

Halawa, Molokaʻi, 2001: Lulu

others could step over it. Lulu had a moment's difficulty, but only because of her flowing raiment. We walked through the field, the high grass twitching with wasps. There was yet another fence around the dark grove itself, but it was made of rotten boughs, and there was a gate without a lock. I pushed open the gate and we entered the labyrinth.

The trees, scarred with nicks from generations of propitiations, were old, the trunks bound with pale strands of desiccated moss. Although it was not the season, one yellow guava glimmered on a tree with mottled bark and spindly arms, its leaves *hinahina,* gray and withered. I had been longing for guavas, like the woman who craved rampion in "Rapunzel." As I went to pick the guava, there was the sound of breaking boughs and a terrible scream. It sounded like a woman in pain; a woman murdered. A long-horned bull pushed his way noisily through the kukuʻi and planted himself, legs splayed, head lowered, before us. I put my hand in my pocket to hold tight to the lock of hair I had cut from my head as an offering, but Kiki, her anklets silent for once beneath her black gown, reached to pick the guava. The wild bull watched us, stiff-legged, moaning with rage. The tree trembled as it resisted her pull, but at last gave up the little fruit with a shudder. John, never taking his eyes from the bull, walked backward through the trees, silently finding his way to the gate which he held open for us.

The guava clutched in her hand, Kiki bounded through the trees, clearing the fence as gracefully as one of the evening deer who stood in the far field, watching us without fear or interest. I dropped the lock of hair as Lulu grabbed my hand. A shrieking bird flitted indignantly above our heads, perhaps the ʻaumakua of Lanikaula, the o'o that cries out in warning when strangers venture too near. The wild bull bellowed in the trees as we ran through the dusk.

We sat on the bank of ferns by the side of the cattle road to catch our breath. John and Kiki would not share the guava, insisting that I have it. Lulu and I ate the guava in four quick bites. Delicious.

I myself have seen it.

Endnotes

CHAPTER 1 THE NIGHT MARCHERS

[1]Harriet Ne, *Tales of Moloka'i,* The Institute for Polynesian Studies, Hawai'i, 1992, pp. 118–20, 139

CHAPTER 2 THE RETURNING GOD

[1]Philip Edwards, ed., *The Journals of Captain Cook,* Penguin, London, 1999, p. 530

[2]E. Alison Kay, "Hawaiian Natural History 1778–1900," *A Natural History of the Hawaiian Islands,* University of Hawaii, Honolulu, 1972, p. 605

[3]Philip Edwards, ed., *The Journals of Captain Cook,* p. 531

[4]Hon. R. M. Daggett, ed., *The Legends and Myths of Hawaii,* His Hawaiian Majesty King David Kalakaua, Mutual Publishing, Honolulu, 1990, p. 26

[5]William Ellis, *Journal of William Ellis,* Advertiser Publishing Co., Honolulu, 1963, p. 2

[6]Philip Edwards, ed., *The Journals of Captain Cook,* p. 534

[7]Maurice Collis, *Cortés and Montezuma,* New Directions, New York, 1954, pp. 55–56

[8]Hon. R. M. Daggett, ed., *The Legends and Myths of Hawaii,* p. 24

[9]Capt. James King, LL.D and F.R.S, *A Voyage to the Pacific etc,* the official Admiralty publication of Cook's 3rd Voyage, Volume III, London, 1784, p. 4

[10]Ibid., p. 7

[11]William Ellis, *Journal of William Ellis,* p. 311

[12]Bernard Smith, *Imagining the Pacific,* Yale University Press, New Haven, 1992, p. 212

[13]Maurice Collis, *Cortés and Montezuma,* pp. 119, 124

[14]Bernal Diaz, *The Conquest of New Spain,* Penguin, London, 1963, p. 220

[15]Maurice Collis, *Cortés and Montezuma,* p. 125

[16]Mary K. Pukui and Alfons L. Korn, trans. and ed., *The Echo of Our Song,* University of Hawaii Press, 1973, p. 6

[17]William Ellis, *Journal of William Ellis,* p. 2

[18]Mircea Eliade, *Myth and Reality,* Harper Torchbooks, New York, 1963, pp. 106–7

[19]C. de B. Evans, trans., *Meister Eckhart,* John M. Watkins, London, 1956, p. 3

[20]Mircea Eliade, *Myth and Reality,* p. 141

[21]Bernard Smith, *Imagining the Pacific,* p. 209

[22]Ibid., p. 231

[23]David W. Forbes, *Encounters with Paradise,* Honolulu Academy of Art, Honolulu, 1992, p. 54

[24]Bernard Smith, *Imagining the Pacific,* p. 212

[25]William Ellis, *Journal of William Ellis,* pp. 83–85

CHAPTER 3 THE EUROPEANS

[1]William Ellis, *Journal of William Ellis,* p. 85

[2]Hon. R. M. Daggett, ed., *The Legends and Myths of Hawaii,* p. 25

[3]Thos. G. Thrum, comp., *Hawaiian Folk Tales,* Mutual Publishing, Honolulu, 1998, p. 26

[4]Philip Edwards, ed., *The Journals of Captain Cook,* pp. 532, 593

[5]Richard Greer, "Dousing Honolulu's Red Lights," *The Hawaiian Journal of History,* Vol. 34, Honolulu Historical Society, Honolulu, 2000, p. 201

[6]Bernard Smith, *Imagining the Pacific,* p. 209

CHAPTER 4 THE GREAT KING

[1]William Ellis, *Journal of William Ellis,* p. 278

[2]Emmett Cahill, *The Life and Times of John Young,* Island Heritage Publishing, Honolulu, 1999, p. 123

[3]Ibid., p. 122

[4]Ibid., p. 124

CHAPTER 5 THE KAPU

[1]Hon. R. M. Daggett, ed., *The Legends and Myths of Hawaii,* p. 437

[2]Ibid., p. 27

[3]John Dominis Holt, *Monarchy in Hawaii,* Ku Pa'a Publishing, Honolulu, 1995, p. 10

[4]William Ellis, *Journal of William Ellis,* pp. 279–80

[5]Jerome Rothenberg, ed., *Technicians of the Sacred,* University of California Press, Berkeley, 1968, p. 409

[6]Hon. R. M. Daggett, ed., *The Legends and Myths of Hawaii,* p. 27

[7]William Ellis, *Journal of William Ellis,* p. 218

[8]Margaret Greer Martin, Nettie Hammond Lyman, Kathryn Lyman Bond and Ethel M. Damon, *The Lymans of Hilo,* Lyman House Memorial Museum, Hilo, 1992, p. 44

CHAPTER 6 THE CHILDREN

[1]John Dominis Holt, *Monarchy in Hawaii,* pp. 4–5, 65

[2]Emmett Cahill, *The Life and Times of John Young,* p. 126

[3]LaRue W. Piercey, *Hawaii's Missionary Saga,* Mutual Publishing, Honolulu, 1992, p. 27

[4]Ibid.

[5]Ibid., p. 31

[6]Ibid., p. 36

[7]Ibid.

[8]Ibid., p. 34

[9]William Ellis, *Journal of William Ellis,* p. 249

[10]LaRue W. Piercey, *Hawaii's Missionary Saga,* p. 20

[11]Bob Krauss, *Here's Hawaii,* Pocket Books, New York, 1960, p. 26

[12]William Ellis, *Journal of William Ellis,* pp. 324–5

[13]Mircea Eliade, *Myth and Reality,* p. 107

[14]William Ellis, *Journal of William Ellis,* p. 223

[15]Ibid., p. 4

[16]John Dominis Holt, *Monarchy in Hawaii,* p. 14

[17]Margaret Greer Martin, et al., *The Lymans of Hilo,* p. 29

[18]John Dominis Holt, *Monarchy in Hawaii,* p. 9

[19]Mary K. Pukui and Alfons L. Korn, trans. and ed., *The Echo of Our Song,* pp. 87–88.

[20]John Dominis Holt, *Monarchy in Hawaii,* pp. 30–31

[21]Samuel H. Elbert and Noelani Mahoe, ed., *Na Mele O Hawaii,* University of Hawaii Press, Honolulu, 1970, p. 68

[22]Margaret Greer Martin, et al., *The Lymans of Hilo,* p. 44

[23]Samuel H. Elbert and Noelani Mahoe, ed., *Na Mele O Hawaii,* p. 17

[24]Ibid., p. 68

[25]Katherine Gerould, *Hawaii Scenes and Impressions,* Charles Scribners' Sons, New York, 1921, p. 14

[26]Martha Beckwith, *The Kumulipo,* University of Chicago Press, Chicago, 1951, p. 7

[27]Caleb Wright, *India and Its Inhabitants,* J. A. Brainerd, Cincinnati, 1853, p. 153

[28]William Ellis, *Journal of William Ellis,* p. 135

[29]Samuel H. Elbert and Noelani Mahoe, ed., *Na Mele O Hawaii,* p. 70

CHAPTER 7 THE ISLANDS

[1]S. H. Sohmer and R. Gustafson, *Plants and Flowers of Hawaii,* University of Hawaii Press, Honolulu, 1987, p. 21

[2]Ibid., pp. 21–22

[3]T. Snell Newman, "Man in the Prehistoric Hawaiian Ecosystem," *A Natural History of the Hawaiian Islands,* University of Hawaii Press, Honolulu, 1972, p. 589

[4]Ibid., p. 585

[5]E. Alison Kay, "Hawaiian Natural History 1778–1900," *A Natural History of the Hawaiian Islands,* p. 610

[6]Mary K. Pukui and Alfons L. Korn, *The Echo of Our Song,* p. 58–59

[7]E. Alison Kay, "Hawaiian Natural History 1778–1900," *A Natural History of the Hawaiian Islands,* p. 618

[8]Ibid, p. 636

[9]Ibid., pp. 636–37

[10]Douglas Boswell, ed., *All About Hawaii,* Star-Bulletin Printing, Honolulu, 1961, p. 15

[11]E. Alison Kay, "Hawaiian Natural History 1778–1900," *A Natural History of the Hawaiian Islands,* p. 608

CHAPTER 8 THE COLLECTORS

[1]Bernard Smith, *Imagining the Pacific,* p. 51

[2]David W. Forbes, *Encounters with Paradise,* p. 77

[3]Ibid., p. 81

[4]Ibid.

[5]Ibid., p. 82

[6]Margaret Greer Martin, et al., *The Lymans of Hilo,* p. 75

[7]Isabella Bird, *Six Months in the Sandwich Islands,* Mutual Publishing, Honolulu, 1998, pp. 182–83

[8]David W. Forbes, *Encounters with Paradise,* p. 77

[9]Hideto Kono and Kazuko Sinoto, "Observations of the First Japanese to Land in Hawaii," *Hawaiian Journal of History,* Vol. 34, Honolulu, 2000, p. 57

[10]Bernard Smith, *Imagining the Pacific,* p. 51

[11]E. Alison Kay, "Hawaiian Natural History 1778–1900," *A Natural History of the Hawaiian Islands,* p. 609

[12]Ibid., p. 616

[13]Ibid., p. 631

[14]Ibid., pp. 625–6

CHAPTER 9 THE MISSIONARY

[1]Margaret Greer Martin, et al., *The Lymans of Hilo,* p. 10

[2]Ibid., p. 39

[3]Ibid., pp. 28, 45

[4]Ibid., pp. 33–34

[5]David W. Forbes, *Encounters with Paradise,* p. 78

[6]Margaret Greer Martin, et al., *The Lymans of Hilo,* p. 57

[7]Ibid., p. 64

[8]Ibid., p. 61

[9]Ibid., p. 83

[10]Ibid., p. 195

CHAPTER 10 THE GENTRY

[1]Jack London, *Tales of Hawaii,* Press Pacifica, Honolulu, 1964, p. 59

[2]Margaret Greer Martin, et al., *The Lymans of Hilo,* p. 145

[3]Katherine Gerould, *Hawaii Scenes and Impressions,* p. 53

[4]Margaret Greer Martin, et al., *The Lymans of Hilo,* pp. 129–30

[5]Ibid. p. 135

[6]Hon. R. M. Daggett, ed., *The Legends and Myths of Hawaii,* p. 29

[7]John Dominis Holt, *Monarchy in Hawaii,* p. 35

[8]Bob Krauss, *Here's Hawaii,* p. 16

[9]Alfons L. Korn, *The Victorian Visitors,* University of Hawaii Press, Honolulu, 1958, p. 58

CHAPTER 11 THE KANAKA MAOLI

[1]Isabella Bird, *Six Months in the Sandwich Islands,* pp. 77, 290

[2]John Dominis Holt, *Monarchy in Hawaii,* p. 36

[3]Mary K. Pukui and Alfons L. Korn, trans. and ed., *The Echo of Our Song,* pp. 154–55

[4]John Dominis Holt, *Monarchy in Hawaii,* pp. 31–32

[5]Ibid., p. 32

[6]Bob Krauss, *Here's Hawaii,* pp. 20–21

[7]Isabella Bird, *Six Months in the Sandwich Islands,* pp. 63–64

[8]John Dominis Holt, *Monarchy in Hawaii,* p. 27

[9]Douglas Boswell, ed., *All about Hawaii,* p. 13

[10]John Dominis Holt, *Monarchy in Hawaii,* p. 25

[11]Mary K. Pukui and Alfons L. Korn, *The Echo of Our Song,* pp. 107–8

[12]Isabella Bird, *Six Months in the Sandwich Islands,* pp. 175–77

[13]John Dominis Holt, *Monarchy in Hawaii,* p. 14

[14]Douglas Boswell, ed., *All about Hawaii,* p. 221

CHAPTER 12 THE QUEEN

[1]John Dominis Holt, *Monarchy in Hawaii,* p. 34

[2]Ibid.

[3]Ibid., p. 37

[4]Samuel H. Elbert and Noelani Mahoe, *Na Mele O Hawaii,* p. 9

[5]Bob Krauss, *Here's Hawaii,* p. 20

[6]Mary K. Pukui and Alfons L. Korn, trans. and ed., *The Echo of Our Song,* pp. 171–2

CHAPTER 13 THE PARADISE

[1]Thos. G. Thrum, comp., *Hawaiian Folk Tales,* p. 138

[2]Kaui Philpotts, *Hawaiian Country Tables,* The Bee Press, Honolulu, 1998, pp. 11, 36, 70, 73

[3]Katherine Gerould, *Hawaii Scenes and Impressions,* p. 44

[4]Ibid., pp. 24, 18

CHAPTER 14 THE MUSICIAN

[1]Thos. G. Thrum, comp., *Hawaiian Folk Tales,* pp. 193, 194, 198–99

[2]William Ellis, *Journal of William Ellis,* pp. 245–6

CHAPTER 15 THE GROVE

[1]W. T. Brigham and Catherine C. Summers, *Moloka'i Site Survey,* Dept. of Anthropology, Bernice Pauahi Bishop Museum, Honolulu, 1971, pp. 167, 169

[2]Ibid., p. 156

[3]Harriet Ne, *Tales of Moloka'i,* p. 63

Acknowledgments

I would like to thank my editor, Larry Porges, who was indispensable, and Jan Morgan of the Kohala Book Shop in Kapaʻau, Hawaiʻi.

ABOUT THE AUTHOR

Susanna Moore was raised in Hawaii and now lives in New York City. She is the author of *In the Cut, Sleeping Beauties, The Whiteness of Bones,* and *My Old Sweetheart.*

This book is set in Garamond 3, designed by
Morris Fuller Benton and Thomas Maitland
Cleland in the 1930s, and Monotype Grotesque,
both released digitally by Adobe.

Printed by R. R. Donnelley and Sons on
Gladfelter 60-pound Thor Offset smooth
white antique paper.

Dust jacket printed by Miken Companies.
Color separation by Quad Graphics.

Three-piece case of Ecological Fiber sand side
panels with Sierra black book cloth as the spine
fabric. Stamped in Lustrofoil metallic silver.

NATIONAL GEOGRAPHIC DIRECTIONS

Featuring works by some of the world's most prominent and highly regarded literary figures, National Geographic Directions captures the spirit of travel and of place for which National Geographic is renowned, bringing fresh perspective and renewed excitement to the art of travel writing.

NATIONAL GEOGRAPHIC DIRECTIONS

Featuring works by some of the world's most prominent and highly regarded literary figures, National Geographic Directions captures the spirit of travel and of place for which National Geographic is renowned, bringing fresh perspective and renewed excitement to the art of travel writing.